S.P DEVDAS

THE POWER

GROW RICH

First published by Zee india bookseller 2024

Copyright © 2024 by S.P Devdas

All rights reserved. No part of this publication may be reproduced, stored or transmitted in any form or by any means, electronic, mechanical, photocopying, recording, scanning, or otherwise without written permission from the publisher. It is illegal to copy this book, post it to a website, or distribute it by any other means without permission.

This novel is entirely a work of fiction. The names, characters and incidents portrayed in it are the work of the author's imagination. Any resemblance to actual persons, living or dead, events or localities is entirely coincidental.

S.P Devdas asserts the moral right to be identified as the author of this work.

S.P Devdas has no responsibility for the persistence or accuracy of URLs for external or third-party Internet Websites referred to in this publication and does not guarantee that any content on such Websites is, or will remain, accurate or appropriate.

Designations used by companies to distinguish their products are often claimed as trademarks. All brand names and product names used in this book and on its cover are trade names, service marks, trademarks and registered trademarks of their respective owners. The publishers and the book are not associated with any product or vendor mentioned in this book. None of the companies referenced within the book have endorsed the book.

First edition

*This book was professionally typeset on Reedsy.
Find out more at reedsy.com*

Contents

1	Introduction: Unveiling the Power Within	1
2	The Genesis of Desire: Fueling Your Ambition	4
3	Setting Your North Star: Defining Your Goals	7
4	The Power of Belief: Cultivating a Success Mindset	10
5	Mastering Your Thoughts: The Foundation of Success	13
6	Turning Defeat into Victory: The Art of Persistence	17
7	The Path of Initiative: Taking Bold Action	20
8	Developing Organized Planning: Blueprint for Success	23
9	Mastering Decision Making: The Bridge to Success	26
10	The Power of the Mastermind: Leveraging Collective...	30
11	Transmuting Sex Energy: Channeling Vitality for Success	34
12	Harnessing the Subconscious Mind: The Hidden Key to Wealth	38
13	The Role of Autosuggestion: Programming Your Success	42
14	Overcoming Fear: Embracing Courage in Adversity	46
15	Building Self-Confidence: The Catalyst for Achievement	51
16	The Power of Imagination: Crafting Your Ideal Future	55
17	Using Specialized Knowledge: The Currency of Experts	58
18	Tapping into the Infinite Intelligence: Connecting with...	62
19	The Power of the Master Mind Alliance: Synergizing with...	65
20	Taking Inspired Action: Seizing Opportunities	68
21	Developing Leadership Skills: Guiding Your Path to Success	71
22	The Power of Enthusiasm: Igniting Passion for Success	76
23	Cultivating Self-Discipline: The Key to Mastery	80
24	Transcending Procrastination: Overcoming Inertia	84
25	Building a Magnetic Personality: Attracting Success	89

26	The Power of Faith: Trusting in Your Vision	93
27	Creating Your Master Plan: Designing Your Destiny	97
28	The Power of Giving: Cultivating Abundance Mentality	101
29	Overcoming Adversity: Turning Challenges into Opportunities	105
30	The Power of Gratitude: Fostering Prosperity Consciousness	109
31	Living Your Legacy: Embracing Fulfillment and Contribution	113
32	"Desire: The Starting Point of All Achievement"	118
33	Faith: Visualizing and Believing in the Attainment of Desire	121
34	Auto-suggestion: The Medium for Influencing the Subconscious...	124
35	Specialized Knowledge: Personalizing Your Path to Success	127
36	Imagination: The Workshop of the Mind	130
37	Organized Planning: Turning Your Ideas into Action Plans	133
38	Decision: The Mastery of Procrastination	137
39	Persistence: The Sustained Effort Necessary to Induce Faith	141
40	The Master Mind: Creating Synergy through Collaboration	146
41	The Mystery of Sex Transmutation: Harnessing Creative Energy	150
42	The Subconscious Mind: Connecting with Your Inner Power	154
43	The Brain: A Broadcasting and Receiving Station for Thought	157
44	The Sixth Sense: The Door to the Temple of Wisdom	161
45	How to Outwit the Six Ghosts of Fear	165
46	The Devil's Workshop: The Power of Negative Thinking	170
47	The Law of Cosmic Habit Force: The Science of Personal...	174
48	How to Develop the "X-Factor": Personal Magnetism	177
49	the "Miracle" of Your Mind: Unlocking Infinite Potential	181
50	How to Transform Failures into Stepping Stones for Success	185
51	The Magic of Enthusiasm: Fueling Your Journey to Greatness	190
52	The Golden Rule: The Principle of Mutual Benefit	194
53	The Four Pillars of Leadership: Defining Your Path to...	198
54	How to Build Self-Confidence and Overcome Self-Consciousness	202
55	The Power of Imagination: Creating Your Reality	207

1

Introduction: Unveiling the Power Within

Welcome to "The Power of Grow Rich," where we embark on a trans formative journey to unlock the boundless potential that resides within each of us. In this introductory chapter, we peel back the layers of doubt and uncertainty to reveal the innate power that lies dormant within our minds and hearts.

Far too often, we underestimate our own abilities, succumbing to the limiting beliefs and societal norms that confine us to mediocrity. But buried beneath the surface lies a reservoir of untapped potential waiting to be unleashed—a power that knows no bounds and holds the key to our ultimate success and fulfillment.

As we embark on this journey together, we will explore the timeless principles and proven strategies that have empowered countless individuals to rise above adversity and achieve greatness. From the depths of despair to the pinnacle of success, the path to riches is paved with unwavering faith, relentless determination, and unwavering commitment to growth.

So, dear reader, prepare to awaken the dormant giant within you. It's time to shatter the shackles of self-doubt and embrace the limitless possibilities that await. The journey ahead may be challenging, but with courage, conviction, and a burning desire to succeed, we will unlock the power of grow rich and transforming our dreams into reality.

Welcome to the journey of self-discovery and empowerment. Within the pages of this book, we embark on a transformative expedition to unlock the latent potential that resides within each of us.

Life, in its vastness and complexity, presents us with endless opportunities and challenges. Yet, amidst the ebb and flow of circumstances, there exists a profound truth: the power to shape our destiny lies within ourselves.

In this introduction, we peel back the layers of doubt and uncertainty to reveal the inherent strength and brilliance that define our essence. We challenge the notion of limitation and embrace the boundless possibilities that await those who dare to dream and take action.

As we delve deeper into the exploration of personal growth and prosperity, we acknowledge the significance of self-awareness and intentionality. By understanding our desires, fears, and aspirations, we gain clarity on the path ahead and unleash the full force of our potential.

But this journey is not without its obstacles. Doubt may creep in, and setbacks may test our resolve. Yet, it is in these moments of adversity that we discover our true resilience and determination.

Through the wisdom of ages past and the insights of modern thought leaders, we illuminate the pathways to success and fulfillment. We draw inspiration from those who have dared to defy convention and chart their own course to greatness.

So, dear reader, as we embark on this odyssey together, I invite you to embrace the power within you. Let us cast aside the shackles of self-doubt and insecurity, and step boldly into the abundant future that awaits. For within each of us lies the potential to achieve greatness and live a life of purpose and passion.

INTRODUCTION: UNVEILING THE POWER WITHIN

2

The Genesis of Desire: Fueling Your Ambition

At the heart of every great achievement lies a burning desire – a relentless spark that ignites the flames of ambition and propels us towards our dreams. In this chapter, we delve into the genesis of desire, exploring its profound influence on our aspirations and actions.

Desire is the primal force that stirs within us, urging us to reach beyond our current circumstances and strive for something greater. It is the seed from which all achievement blossoms, the driving force behind every innovation, invention, and breakthrough.

But what is desire, and how does it manifest in our lives? It is more than a fleeting whim or passing fancy; it is a deep longing, an unyielding hunger that compels us to pursue our goals with unwavering determination.

Desire is born from the recognition of possibility – the belief that we are capable of transcending our limitations and achieving the extraordinary. It is fueled by passion, fueled by a burning desire to create, to contribute, to leave our mark on the world.

Yet, desire alone is not enough. It must be coupled with clarity of purpose and unwavering commitment. It is not merely wishful thinking, but a steadfast commitment to action – a willingness to do whatever it takes to turn our dreams into reality.

THE GENESIS OF DESIRE: FUELING YOUR AMBITION

In this chapter, we explore the art of nurturing desire, cultivating it like a precious seedling until it grows into a mighty oak. We examine the role of vision, goal setting, and visualization in harnessing the power of desire and channeling it towards our objectives.

We also confront the obstacles that stand in the way of our desires – the doubts, fears, and limiting beliefs that threaten to extinguish the flames of ambition. Through the power of self-awareness and positive thinking, we learn to overcome these barriers and unleash the full force of our potential.

So, dear reader, I invite you to embrace your desires, to nurture them with care and attention, and to unleash their power to fuel your ambition. For within the depths of your soul lies the spark of greatness – a flame waiting to be ignited.

Desire is the spark that ignites the flames of ambition, propelling us forward on our journey toward success. It is the magnetic force that draws us toward our dreams, compelling us to pursue them with unwavering determination.

In this chapter, we delve into the genesis of desire and explore its profound influence on our lives. From the deepest recesses of our being, desire emerges as a primal force, urging us to aspire for more, to reach beyond the confines of our current reality.

But what exactly is desire? It is more than a mere wish or fleeting thought; it is a burning passion that fuels our actions and drives us toward our goals. It is the relentless pursuit of excellence, the unyielding commitment to realize our fullest potential.

At its core, desire is deeply intertwined with our values, beliefs, and aspirations. It is shaped by our experiences, shaped by our desires, and shaped by our desires. It is the force that propels us forward, guiding our decisions and shaping our destiny.

Yet, desire alone is not enough. It must be accompanied by clarity of purpose and unwavering commitment. It requires us to define our goals with precision and to cultivate the resilience to overcome obstacles along the way.

In the pursuit of our desires, we may encounter doubt, fear, and uncertainty. But it is in these moments of challenge that our resolve is truly tested. It is when we summon the courage to confront our fears and press forward in the face of adversity that we demonstrate our true strength.

So, dear reader, I urge you to embrace your desires with courage and conviction. Let them serve as the guiding light on your journey toward greatness. For it is through the pursuit of our deepest desires that we unlock the full potential of our lives and create a legacy that will endure for generations to come.

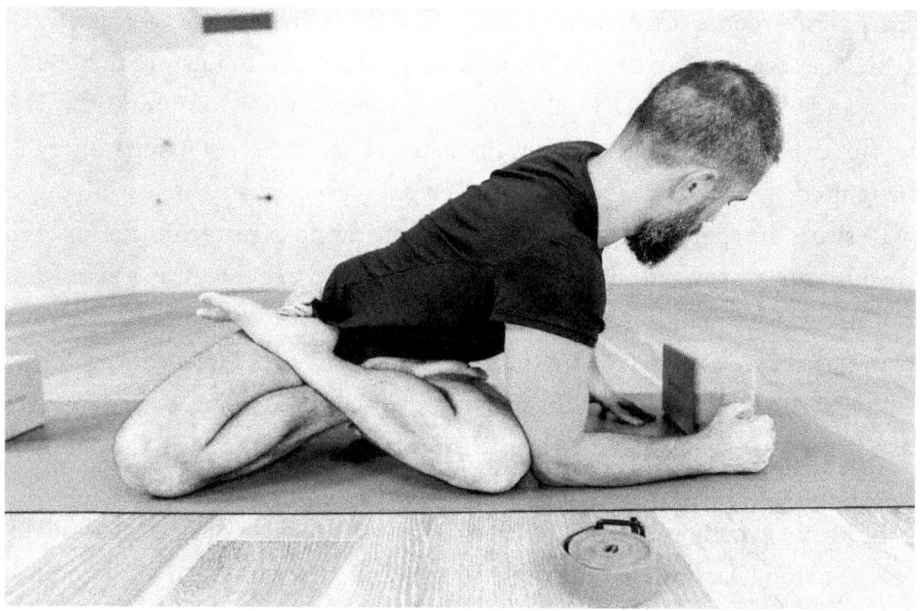

3

3

Setting Your North Star: Defining Your Goals

I n the vast expanse of life's journey, goals serve as our guiding stars, illuminating the path ahead and steering us toward our desired destination. Like a ship navigating the open seas, having a clear North Star ensures that we stay on course, even in the face of turbulent waters and uncertain skies.

But what exactly are goals? They are not just fleeting desires or whimsical fantasies; they are concrete milestones that we strive to achieve. They provide us with direction, purpose, and a sense of meaning in our pursuit of success and fulfillment.

In this chapter, we delve into the importance of setting goals and the profound impact they have on our lives. We explore the process of defining our aspirations with clarity and intentionality, ensuring that they are aligned with our values, passions, and long-term vision.

Setting goals is more than just scribbling down a list of wishes; it is a deliberate and systematic process that requires careful consideration and planning. It involves identifying what truly matters to us and committing to taking actionable steps to turn our dreams into reality.

When setting goals, it is essential to make them specific, measurable, achievable, relevant, and time-bound – often referred to as the SMART criteria. By doing so, we increase our chances of success and maintain focus and momentum as we progress toward our objectives.

Moreover, setting goals allows us to tap into the power of visualization and positive affirmation. By vividly imagining ourselves achieving our goals and affirming our ability to do so, we prime our minds for success and cultivate a mindset of abundance and possibility.

Yet, as we embark on the journey of goal setting, we must remain flexible and adaptable to change. Life is unpredictable, and circumstances may evolve over time, requiring us to adjust our goals accordingly. By remaining open-minded and resilient, we can navigate obstacles and seize new opportunities as they arise.

So, dear reader, I encourage you to set your North Star high and chart a course toward your dreams. Let your goals be the compass that guides you through life's adventures, guiding you toward a future filled with purpose, passion, and prosperity.

In the vast expanse of life's journey, our goals act as guiding stars, illuminating the path we traverse and directing our efforts toward meaningful destinations. Much like a mariner relies on the North Star to navigate the seas, setting clear goals provides us with direction and purpose.

In this chapter, we explore the significance of defining our goals and charting a course toward their attainment. Just as a ship without a destination drifts aimlessly, a life without goals lacks direction and fulfillment.

But what exactly are goals? They are the tangible manifestations of our aspirations, the milestones that mark our progress, and the benchmarks by which we measure our success. Whether they be personal, professional, or spiritual, goals serve as beacons of light, guiding us toward the fulfillment of our deepest desires.

The process of setting goals begins with introspection and reflection. It requires us to delve deep within ourselves to unearth our passions, values, and dreams. By clarifying what truly matters to us, we can set goals that resonate with our authentic selves and inspire us to take action.

Moreover, goals must be SMART: specific, measurable, achievable, relevant, and time-bound. By articulating our goals in this manner, we provide ourselves with a clear roadmap for success and ensure that our efforts are focused and purposeful.

Yet, setting goals is not merely an intellectual exercise; it is a deeply personal and transformative process. It requires us to confront our fears, overcome our doubts, and step outside of our comfort zones. But it is through this process of growth and self-discovery that we unlock our true potential and become the architects of our own destiny.

So, dear reader, I encourage you to set your North Star high and strive toward its brilliance with unwavering determination. For it is through the pursuit of our goals that we realize our fullest potential and embark on a journey of purpose and fulfillment.

4

4

The Power of Belief: Cultivating a Success Mindset

Belief is the cornerstone of achievement, the driving force behind every great endeavor. It is the unwavering faith in ourselves and our abilities that propels us forward in the face of adversity and empowers us to turn our dreams into reality.

In this chapter, we explore the profound impact of belief on our mindset and our ability to succeed. From the moment we conceive an idea to the moment we achieve our goals, belief serves as the catalyst that transforms possibility into probability.

At its essence, belief is a deeply ingrained conviction that we can accomplish that which we set out to do. It is the inner voice that whispers words of encouragement in times of doubt and spurs us onward when the path ahead seems daunting.

But belief is more than just positive thinking; it is a fundamental shift in perspective that shapes our reality. When we believe in ourselves and our capacity to succeed, we exude confidence and resilience, attracting opportunities and overcoming obstacles with ease.

Moreover, belief is contagious. When we radiate confidence and conviction, we inspire those around us to believe in themselves and their potential. In this way, belief becomes a powerful force for positive change, uplifting individuals and communities alike.

Yet, belief is not immune to doubt and skepticism. In our journey toward success, we may encounter setbacks and challenges that shake our faith and test our resolve. But it is in these moments of uncertainty that our belief is truly put to the test. It is when we choose to persevere in the face of adversity that we affirm our commitment to our goals and reaffirm our belief in ourselves.

So, dear reader, I urge you to cultivate a success mindset rooted in unwavering belief. Trust in yourself and your abilities, and embrace the limitless potential that resides within you. For it is through the power of belief that we transform our dreams into reality and create a life of purpose, passion, and fulfillment.

Belief is the cornerstone of achievement, the fertile soil from which our dreams take root and flourish. It is the unwavering confidence in our abilities, the steadfast conviction that we are capable of overcoming any obstacle on the path to success.

In this chapter, we delve into the profound impact of belief on our lives and explore strategies for cultivating a success mindset. For it is through the power of belief that we unlock our full potential and manifest our greatest aspirations.

Belief is more than just positive thinking; it is a deep-seated conviction that permeates every aspect of our being. It shapes our thoughts, influences our actions, and ultimately determines our destiny. When we believe in ourselves and our ability to succeed, we tap into a reservoir of inner strength and resilience that propels us forward in the face of adversity.

But belief is not always easy to cultivate, especially in the face of doubt and uncertainty. It requires us to challenge the limiting beliefs that hold us back and replace them with empowering thoughts and affirmations. By consciously choosing to focus on the positive and banish self-doubt, we reprogram our minds for success and create a fertile environment for growth.

Moreover, belief is contagious. When we believe in ourselves, we inspire others to believe in us as well. By radiating confidence and optimism, we attract opportunities and allies who support us on our journey to greatness.

In cultivating a success mindset, it is essential to surround ourselves with positivity and inspiration. Whether through books, mentors, or affirmations, we must nourish our minds with uplifting thoughts and ideas that reinforce our belief in our ability to succeed.

So, dear reader, I urge you to cultivate the power of belief in your life. Trust in yourself and your dreams, and let your unwavering faith be the driving force behind your journey to success. For when you believe in yourself, anything is possible.

5

5

Mastering Your Thoughts: The Foundation of Success

Our thoughts are the architects of our reality, shaping the world around us and influencing the outcomes we experience. In the grand symphony of life, they are the conductor, orchestrating the melody of our existence.

In this chapter, we delve into the profound impact of mastering our thoughts and explore how they serve as the foundation of success. For it is through the mastery of our inner world that we unlock the power to create the life of our dreams.

Our thoughts possess an incredible creative power. They have the ability to mold our perceptions, shape our beliefs, and ultimately determine our actions. When we harness this power and learn to direct our thoughts toward positive and empowering outcomes, we set the stage for success.

Yet, mastering our thoughts is no easy feat. It requires discipline, self-awareness, and a commitment to continuous growth. It means taking ownership of our inner dialogue and consciously choosing to focus on thoughts that uplift and inspire us.

One of the most powerful tools in mastering our thoughts is mindfulness. By cultivating present-moment awareness, we gain insight into the patterns of our thinking and can begin to observe our thoughts without judgment. In doing so, we create space for greater clarity and intentionality in our actions.

Moreover, mastering our thoughts requires us to challenge the limiting beliefs and negative self-talk that hold us back. By reframing our perspectives and choosing to see obstacles as opportunities for growth, we empower ourselves to overcome challenges and achieve our goals.

In mastering our thoughts, it is essential to cultivate a mindset of abundance and possibility. By focusing on what we want to create rather than what we fear, we open ourselves up to a world of endless potential and opportunity.

So, dear reader, I encourage you to embark on the journey of mastering your thoughts. Take control of your inner narrative, and let your thoughts be a reflection of the success and abundance you wish to experience in your life. For it is through the power of our thoughts that we shape our destiny and create the life of our dreams.

Our thoughts are the architects of our reality, the blueprint upon which our lives are built. They shape our perceptions, influence our emotions, and ultimately determine our actions. In this chapter, we explore the profound impact of mastering our thoughts and how it serves as the foundation of success.

At the core of mastering our thoughts lies the principle of mindfulness - the practice of consciously observing and directing our mental processes. By becoming aware of our thoughts, we gain insight into their origins and can choose to cultivate those that serve our goals and discard those that do not.

Thought mastery begins with self-awareness. It requires us to pay attention to the patterns and tendencies of our thinking and to recognize the beliefs and biases that shape our perceptions. Through introspection and reflection, we can identify any negative or limiting thoughts that may be holding us back and replace them with positive and empowering ones.

Moreover, mastering our thoughts involves learning to control the quality of our mental discourse. Instead of allowing our minds to wander aimlessly or dwell on worries and anxieties, we can consciously direct our thoughts toward productive and constructive ends. By focusing on solutions rather than problems, we empower ourselves to take proactive steps toward our goals.

MASTERING YOUR THOUGHTS: THE FOUNDATION OF SUCCESS

One of the most powerful tools for mastering our thoughts is the practice of affirmations. By repeatedly affirming positive statements about ourselves and our abilities, we reprogram our subconscious minds for success and create a mental environment conducive to achievement.

Additionally, mastering our thoughts requires us to cultivate a mindset of abundance rather than scarcity. Instead of dwelling on what we lack, we can train ourselves to focus on the abundance of opportunities and resources available to us. By adopting an abundance mindset, we open ourselves up to new possibilities and attract success into our lives.

In essence, mastering our thoughts is the key to unlocking our full potential and achieving our greatest aspirations. By taking control of our mental processes and directing them toward positive ends, we lay the foundation for success in all areas of our lives. So, dear reader, I encourage you to embark on the journey of thought mastery and harness the immense power of your mind to create the life you desire.

6

6

Turning Defeat into Victory: The Art of Persistence

Defeat is not the end but a stepping stone on the path to victory. In this chapter, we delve into the transformative power of persistence, the unwavering determination to persevere in the face of adversity, and emerge stronger and more resilient than before.

At some point in our lives, we all encounter setbacks and failures. These moments can be disheartening, testing our resolve and shaking our confidence. However, it is how we respond to defeat that ultimately determines our success.

Persistence is the refusal to surrender in the face of obstacles. It is the willingness to pick ourselves up, dust ourselves off, and continue onward, despite the challenges that may arise. It is the understanding that failure is not a reflection of our worth but an opportunity for growth and learning.

The art of persistence begins with a mindset shift. Instead of viewing failure as a final verdict, we must see it as a temporary setback, a detour on the road to success. By reframing our perspective, we can extract valuable lessons from our experiences and use them to fuel our journey forward.

Moreover, persistence requires resilience - the ability to bounce back from adversity and keep moving forward. It is the courage to face our fears and doubts head-on, knowing that with each step we take, we inch closer to our goals.

One of the most powerful examples of persistence in action is the story of Thomas Edison, who famously said, "I have not failed. I've just found 10,000 ways that won't work." Despite numerous setbacks, Edison persisted in his quest to invent the electric light bulb, eventually achieving success through sheer determination and perseverance.

In our own lives, we can draw inspiration from Edison's example and embrace the mindset of persistence. Whether we face rejection in our careers, setbacks in our relationships, or challenges in our personal growth, we can choose to see these experiences as opportunities to grow and evolve.

So, dear reader, I encourage you to embrace the art of persistence in your own life. Remember that every setback is a chance to rise stronger, wiser, and more determined than before. With persistence as your guiding light, you can turn defeat into victory and achieve the success you desire.

Defeat is not the end of the road; rather, it is a temporary setback on the journey to success. In this chapter, we explore the transformative power of persistence in overcoming adversity and turning defeat into victory.

At some point in our lives, we all encounter setbacks, failures, and disappointments. These challenges can be disheartening and demoralizing, causing us to question our abilities and our worth. However, it is how we respond to these setbacks that ultimately determines our fate.

The art of persistence lies in our ability to bounce back from defeat, to dust ourselves off and continue moving forward in the face of adversity. It is the refusal to accept failure as final and the unwavering commitment to persevere until we achieve our goals.

One of the key ingredients of persistence is resilience - the ability to withstand adversity and bounce back stronger than before. Resilient individuals view setbacks as opportunities for growth and learning, rather than insurmountable obstacles. They draw strength from their failures and use them as stepping stones to future success.

Moreover, persistence requires a clear sense of purpose and vision. When we are deeply committed to our goals and passionate about our dreams, we are willing to endure any hardship or setback in order to achieve them. Our vision becomes our guiding light, leading us through the darkest of times and inspiring us to keep going, no matter what.

Persistence also involves the willingness to adapt and evolve in the face of changing circumstances. Rather than stubbornly clinging to a single course of action, we remain flexible and open-minded, willing to adjust our strategies as needed in order to overcome obstacles and achieve our objectives.

In the words of Winston Churchill, "Success is not final, failure is not fatal: It is the courage to continue that counts." Indeed, true success is not measured by the absence of failure, but by our ability to persist in the face of it. So, dear reader, I encourage you to embrace the art of persistence in your own life and turn every defeat into a stepping stone on the path to victory.

7

The Path of Initiative: Taking Bold Action

Initiative is the catalyst that propels us from contemplation to realization, from aspiration to achievement. In this chapter, we explore the transformative power of taking bold action and seizing control of our destiny.

At the heart of the path of initiative lies the willingness to step forward and take charge of our lives. It is the recognition that we are the architects of our own fate, and that our destiny is shaped by the choices we make and the actions we take.

Taking initiative requires courage - the courage to step outside of our comfort zones, to confront our fears, and to embrace uncertainty. It means pushing past the boundaries of what is familiar and safe in order to pursue our dreams and aspirations.

But initiative is more than just bravery; it is also about vision and determination. It is about having a clear sense of purpose and direction, and the resolve to persevere in the face of obstacles and challenges.

Moreover, taking bold action requires a willingness to accept responsibility for our choices and their consequences. It means owning our successes and failures alike, and learning from each experience to become stronger and more resilient.

One of the most powerful aspects of initiative is its ability to inspire others. When we take bold action and pursue our dreams with passion and conviction, we become beacons of inspiration for those around us. We show others what is possible when we dare to dream big and take decisive steps toward our goals.

In essence, the path of initiative is about taking control of our lives and refusing to be passive bystanders in our own stories. It is about seizing the reins of destiny and forging our own path, regardless of the challenges that may lie ahead.

So, dear reader, I encourage you to embrace the path of initiative in your own life. Take bold action, pursue your dreams with passion and determination, and seize control of your destiny. For it is through taking initiative that we create the lives we truly desire and become the architects of our own happiness and fulfillment.

Initiative is the catalyst that propels us from contemplation to action, from dreams to reality. In this chapter, we delve into the importance of seizing initiative and taking bold action in pursuit of our goals and aspirations.

At the heart of the path of initiative lies the willingness to step outside our comfort zones and into the realm of uncertainty. It requires courage, determination, and a willingness to embrace risk in order to make progress and achieve our desires.

Taking initiative means being proactive rather than reactive, actively seeking out opportunities and solutions rather than waiting for them to come to us. It's about taking ownership of our lives and refusing to be passive bystanders in our own stories.

Moreover, initiative is closely linked to innovation and creativity. By taking bold action and exploring new possibilities, we push the boundaries of what is possible and pave the way for new discoveries and breakthroughs.

Initiative also requires a willingness to learn and grow from failure. Not every action we take will lead to success, but each failure brings with it valuable lessons and insights that can inform our future endeavors. By embracing failure as a natural part of the journey, we develop resilience and fortitude, making us better equipped to tackle challenges in the future.

In taking bold action and seizing initiative, we not only realize our own potential but also inspire others to do the same. Our actions serve as a beacon of hope and possibility, showing others what is possible when we dare to dream and take action.

So, dear reader, I urge you to embrace the path of initiative in your own life. Dare to take bold action, step outside your comfort zone, and pursue your goals with unwavering determination. For it is through taking initiative that we truly unleash our potential and create the life we desire.

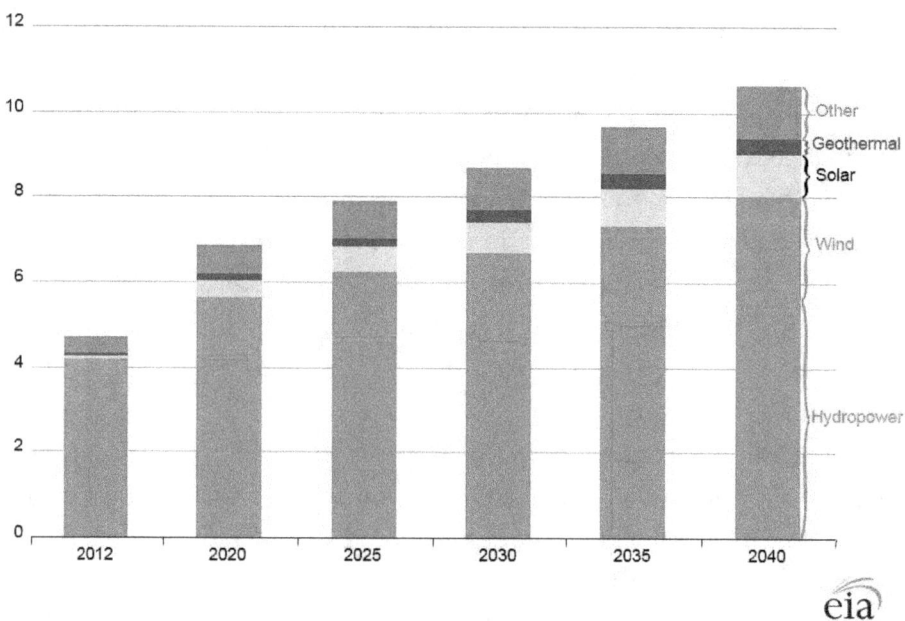

Figure 5-4. World net electricity generation from renewable power by fuel, 2012–40
trillion kilowatthours

8

8

Developing Organized Planning: Blueprint for Success

In the pursuit of our dreams and aspirations, organized planning serves as the blueprint that guides us toward success. In this chapter, we explore the critical role that structured planning plays in achieving our goals and fulfilling our potential.

Organized planning begins with a clear vision of what we want to achieve. It requires us to define our goals with precision and clarity, breaking them down into manageable steps that can be executed systematically.

A well-crafted plan serves as a roadmap for our journey, providing direction and guidance as we navigate the challenges and opportunities that lie ahead. It helps us to stay focused and disciplined, ensuring that our actions are aligned with our objectives.

Moreover, organized planning allows us to anticipate potential obstacles and devise strategies for overcoming them. By conducting thorough research and analysis, we can identify potential risks and pitfalls and develop contingency plans to mitigate them.

One of the key elements of organized planning is setting priorities. It's essential to identify the tasks and activities that will have the greatest impact on our goals and focus our time and energy on them. By prioritizing effectively, we can maximize our productivity and make steady progress toward our objectives.

Furthermore, organized planning involves creating a timeline for our actions and setting deadlines for their completion. This helps to create a sense of urgency and accountability, motivating us to take consistent action and stay on track toward our goals.

In essence, organized planning is the foundation upon which success is built. By taking the time to define our goals, develop a strategic plan, and execute it with discipline and determination, we set ourselves up for success and create a pathway to our dreams.

So, dear reader, I encourage you to embrace the power of organized planning in your own life. Take the time to clarify your goals, develop a detailed plan of action, and commit yourself wholeheartedly to its execution. For with organized planning as your guide, there is no limit to what you can achieve.

Organized planning serves as the bedrock upon which our aspirations are transformed into tangible reality. In this chapter, we delve into the pivotal role of structured planning as the blueprint for success.

At its essence, organized planning is the deliberate process of charting a course of action to achieve our goals. It involves setting clear objectives, devising strategies, and allocating resources in a systematic manner to ensure progress and productivity.

One of the fundamental aspects of organized planning is goal setting. By defining specific, measurable, achievable, relevant, and time-bound objectives, we create a roadmap for success that guides our actions and keeps us focused on what truly matters.

Moreover, organized planning requires careful analysis and assessment of our current circumstances and resources. By conducting a thorough inventory of our strengths, weaknesses, opportunities, and threats, we gain valuable insights into the challenges and opportunities that lie ahead, allowing us to plan accordingly.

Another crucial component of organized planning is the creation of actionable steps and timelines. Breaking down our goals into smaller, manageable tasks not only makes them more achievable but also provides

DEVELOPING ORGANIZED PLANNING: BLUEPRINT FOR SUCCESS

us with a sense of direction and momentum as we progress toward our objectives.

Furthermore, organized planning involves the effective allocation of resources, including time, money, and energy. By prioritizing tasks and making efficient use of available resources, we maximize our productivity and optimize our chances of success.

In essence, organized planning is the cornerstone of success, providing us with the structure and discipline needed to turn our dreams into reality. By following a well-defined plan and remaining committed to our goals, we position ourselves for long-term growth and prosperity.

So, dear reader, I encourage you to embrace the power of organized planning in your own life. Take the time to define your goals, devise a clear strategy, and execute your plan with determination and perseverance. For it is through organized planning that we lay the foundation for success and achieve our fullest potential.

9

9

Mastering Decision Making: The Bridge to Success

Decision-making is the bridge that connects our aspirations to their realization, guiding us from contemplation to action. In this chapter, we explore the pivotal role of effective decision-making as the linchpin of success.

At its core, mastering decision-making involves the art of discerning between alternatives and choosing the path that aligns most closely with our goals and values. It is a skill that requires clarity of purpose, critical thinking, and a willingness to take calculated risks.

One of the key aspects of mastering decision-making is understanding the importance of timing. Often, the success or failure of a decision hinges on making it at the right moment. By carefully considering the relevant factors and assessing the potential outcomes, we increase our chances of making sound decisions that propel us toward our objectives.

Moreover, effective decision-making requires us to embrace uncertainty and ambiguity. In today's fast-paced world, we are often faced with incomplete information and rapidly changing circumstances. By cultivating a mindset of flexibility and adaptability, we can make informed decisions even in the face of uncertainty, adjusting our course as needed to stay on track toward our goals.

Another critical component of mastering decision-making is considering the long-term implications of our choices. While it may be tempting to prioritize short-term gains, true success often requires us to make decisions that are aligned with our overarching goals and values. By taking a holistic view and considering the potential consequences of our actions, we can make decisions that serve us well in the long run.

Furthermore, mastering decision-making involves learning from our past experiences and mistakes. Every decision we make provides us with an opportunity to learn and grow, regardless of the outcome. By reflecting on our decisions and evaluating their impact, we can hone our decision-making skills and become more adept at navigating the complexities of life.

In essence, mastering decision-making is the key to unlocking our full potential and achieving our goals. By cultivating clarity, embracing uncertainty, and learning from our experiences, we can make informed decisions that propel us toward success and fulfillment.

So, dear reader, I encourage you to embrace the art of decision-making in your own life. Take the time to weigh your options, consider the potential outcomes, and trust your instincts. For it is through mastering decision-making that we build the bridge to success and create the life we desire.

Decisions are the building blocks of our destiny, shaping the trajectory of our lives and paving the way to success. In this chapter, we explore the art of mastering decision-making as the crucial bridge between where we are and where we aspire to be.

At its core, decision-making is the process of choosing between alternative courses of action. Whether big or small, each decision we make has the potential to impact our lives in profound ways. Therefore, mastering this skill is essential for navigating the complexities of life and achieving our goals.

One of the key elements of effective decision-making is clarity of purpose. Before making any decision, it's important to have a clear understanding of our goals, values, and priorities. This clarity provides us with a guiding light, helping us to align our decisions with our long-term aspirations.

Moreover, mastering decision-making requires the ability to gather and evaluate relevant information. By seeking out diverse perspectives, weighing the pros and cons, and considering the potential consequences of each option, we empower ourselves to make informed and thoughtful choices.

Another critical aspect of decision-making is trusting our intuition. While rational analysis is important, there are times when our instincts can provide valuable insights that logic alone cannot. Learning to listen to our inner voice and trusting our gut feelings can lead to more authentic and fulfilling decisions.

Furthermore, mastering decision-making involves embracing uncertainty and taking calculated risks. Not every decision will have a guaranteed outcome, and there may be times when we need to step outside our comfort zones and embrace the unknown in order to grow and succeed.

In essence, mastering decision-making is about taking ownership of our choices and accepting responsibility for the consequences. By cultivating clarity, gathering information, trusting our intuition, and embracing uncertainty, we empower ourselves to make decisions that align with our values and lead us closer to our goals.

So, dear reader, I encourage you to embrace the art of mastering decision-making in your own life. Approach each decision with intentionality, gather the necessary information, trust your instincts, and be willing to take calculated risks. For it is through mastering this essential skill that we build the bridge to success and create the life we desire.

MASTERING DECISION MAKING: THE BRIDGE TO SUCCESS

10

10

The Power of the Mastermind: Leveraging Collective Intelligence

The concept of the mastermind is a testament to the profound truth that we are stronger together than we are alone. In this chapter, we explore the transformative potential of harnessing collective intelligence and the synergy that arises when like-minded individuals come together in pursuit of common goals.

At its core, a mastermind is a collective of individuals who come together with a shared purpose, a commitment to mutual growth, and a willingness to support and uplift one another. It is a forum for collaboration, brainstorming, and idea-sharing, where each member brings their unique perspective and expertise to the table.

One of the most powerful aspects of the mastermind is its ability to generate new insights and perspectives that would be impossible to achieve in isolation. By pooling together the collective wisdom, experience, and creativity of its members, a mastermind can unlock innovative solutions to even the most complex challenges.

Moreover, the mastermind serves as a source of accountability and encouragement, motivating its members to stay focused on their goals and take consistent action toward their aspirations. The shared commitment to growth and success creates a supportive environment where each member feels empowered to strive for excellence.

In addition, the mastermind provides a platform for networking and collaboration, opening doors to new opportunities and connections that can propel members toward their goals. By surrounding themselves with ambitious and like-minded individuals, members of a mastermind can expand their professional networks and tap into valuable resources and expertise.

Furthermore, the mastermind fosters a culture of generosity and reciprocity, where members freely share their knowledge, skills, and connections for the benefit of the group as a whole. This spirit of collaboration and cooperation not only accelerates the growth and success of individual members but also contributes to the collective advancement of the entire group.

In essence, the power of the mastermind lies in its ability to leverage the collective intelligence and energy of its members to achieve extraordinary results. By coming together with a shared purpose and a commitment to mutual support and growth, members of a mastermind can unlock their full potential and create positive change in their lives and in the world.

So, dear reader, I encourage you to seek out or create your own mastermind group. Surround yourself with individuals who share your vision and values, and together, unleash the power of collective intelligence to achieve your goals and aspirations.

In the journey towards success, the individual mind is potent, but the collective mind is transformational. In this chapter, we delve into the profound impact of the mastermind concept and how leveraging collective intelligence can propel us towards greater heights of achievement.

At its core, a mastermind is a group of individuals who come together with a shared purpose, pooling their knowledge, skills, and resources to support one another's goals and aspirations. The power of the mastermind lies in its ability to harness the collective wisdom and energy of its members, amplifying the potential for innovation, growth, and success.

One of the key benefits of participating in a mastermind is the opportunity for collaborative learning and brainstorming. By engaging in open dialogue and exchanging ideas with others who share our interests and ambitions, we gain fresh perspectives and insights that can inspire breakthroughs and fuel our progress.

Moreover, a mastermind provides a supportive environment where members can challenge and encourage one another to reach new heights of achievement. The accountability and camaraderie fostered within a mastermind group create a sense of shared responsibility and commitment to each other's success.

Another advantage of the mastermind is the opportunity for networking and collaboration. By connecting with individuals from diverse backgrounds and industries, we expand our professional network and open doors to new opportunities for collaboration, partnership, and growth.

Furthermore, a mastermind can serve as a source of motivation and inspiration during challenging times. By surrounding ourselves with like-minded individuals who are committed to personal and professional growth, we draw strength and encouragement from their enthusiasm and resilience.

In essence, the power of the mastermind lies in its ability to create synergy - the whole becomes greater than the sum of its parts. By harnessing the collective intelligence, creativity, and energy of its members, a mastermind group becomes a dynamic force for positive change and transformation.

So, dear reader, I encourage you to seek out opportunities to participate in or create your own mastermind group. Surround yourself with individuals who share your vision and aspirations, and leverage the power of collective intelligence to propel yourself towards greater success and fulfillment.

11

11

Transmuting Sex Energy: Channeling Vitality for Success

Sexual energy is a potent force that, when harnessed and directed purposefully, can fuel our journey towards success and fulfillment. In this chapter, we explore the transformative practice of transmuting sexual energy and channeling its vitality towards our goals.

At its essence, transmutation is the process of converting one form of energy into another. When it comes to sexual energy, rather than allowing it to dissipate through fleeting desires or uncontrolled impulses, we can consciously redirect it towards more productive endeavors.

One of the most powerful ways to transmute sexual energy is through creative expression. By channeling our passion and vitality into creative pursuits such as art, music, writing, or entrepreneurship, we tap into a wellspring of inspiration and innovation that can propel us towards our goals.

Moreover, physical exercise and movement can serve as a powerful outlet for transmuting sexual energy. Engaging in activities such as yoga, dance, or martial arts not only helps to release tension and stress but also channels our primal energy into physical vitality and strength.

Additionally, spiritual practices such as meditation, mindfulness, and breathwork can aid in the process of transmutation by helping us to cultivate awareness and presence in the moment. By connecting with our innermost selves and tapping into the deeper reservoirs of our being, we can harness the transformative power of sexual energy to fuel our spiritual growth and evolution.

Furthermore, transmuting sexual energy involves cultivating healthy relationships and connections with others. By fostering intimacy, trust, and mutual respect in our interactions, we create a supportive and nurturing environment that allows us to channel our energy towards shared goals and aspirations.

In essence, transmuting sexual energy is about harnessing the primal vitality within us and channeling it towards our highest aspirations. By embracing this transformative practice, we unlock a reservoir of power and potential that can propel us towards greater success, fulfillment, and vitality in all areas of our lives.

So, dear reader, I encourage you to explore the practice of transmuting sexual energy in your own life. Whether through creative expression, physical exercise, spiritual practice, or meaningful relationships, find ways to harness the power of your vitality and channel it towards your goals and dreams.

Sexual energy is a potent force that, when harnessed and directed effectively, can fuel our pursuits and elevate our achievements. In this chapter, we explore the transformative practice of transmuting sexual energy and channeling it towards success in various aspects of life.

Sexual energy is a primal force that resides within each of us, imbuing us with vitality, creativity, and drive. When left unchecked or misdirected, it can lead to distraction, impulsivity, and unfulfilled desires. However, when consciously harnessed and channeled, it can become a powerful source of motivation, focus, and inspiration.

One of the key principles of transmuting sexual energy is the cultivation of self-awareness and self-control. By becoming attuned to our desires and impulses, we can learn to channel and redirect our sexual energy towards more constructive pursuits, such as creative endeavors, career advancement, or personal growth.

Moreover, transmuting sexual energy involves the practice of sublimation

- the process of transforming raw instinctual urges into higher forms of expression. By channeling our sexual energy into activities that align with our goals and values, we can harness its inherent power to fuel our ambitions and propel us towards success.

Another aspect of transmuting sexual energy is the cultivation of physical, mental, and emotional well-being. By engaging in practices such as exercise, meditation, and mindfulness, we can balance and harmonize our energy centers, allowing us to tap into our full potential and operate at peak performance levels.

Furthermore, transmuting sexual energy involves the cultivation of healthy relationships and connections. By fostering meaningful connections with others based on trust, respect, and mutual support, we can create a supportive environment that nurtures our growth and success.

In essence, transmuting sexual energy is about harnessing the inherent power within us and directing it towards our highest aspirations. By cultivating self-awareness, practicing sublimation, nurturing well-being, and fostering meaningful connections, we can unleash the full potential of our sexual energy and channel it towards success in all areas of life.

So, dear reader, I encourage you to explore the practice of transmuting sexual energy in your own life. Embrace your vitality, harness your drive, and channel your passion towards realizing your dreams and aspirations. For when we learn to master our sexual energy, we unlock a potent source of vitality and inspiration that can propel us towards greater success and fulfillment.

TRANSMUTING SEX ENERGY: CHANNELING VITALITY FOR SUCCESS

12

12

Harnessing the Subconscious Mind: The Hidden Key to Wealth

The subconscious mind is a reservoir of untapped potential, holding the keys to unlocking wealth and prosperity. In this chapter, we explore the profound impact of harnessing the subconscious mind and how it serves as the hidden key to unlocking abundance in our lives.

Deep within the recesses of our minds lies the subconscious - a vast reservoir of beliefs, memories, and patterns that shape our thoughts, emotions, and behaviors. While the conscious mind may govern our rational thinking and decision-making, it is the subconscious mind that holds the power to manifest our deepest desires and aspirations.

One of the key principles of harnessing the subconscious mind is the practice of positive affirmation and visualization. By affirming our goals and desires in a positive and present tense, we send powerful signals to the subconscious, instructing it to align our thoughts and actions with our intentions. Through visualization, we vividly imagine ourselves achieving our goals, thereby programming our subconscious to work tirelessly towards their realization.

Moreover, harnessing the subconscious mind involves the cultivation of a mindset of abundance and prosperity. By replacing limiting beliefs and scarcity mentality with thoughts of abundance and wealth, we create a fertile mental environment that attracts prosperity and opportunities into our lives.

Another aspect of harnessing the subconscious mind is the practice of mindfulness and meditation. By quieting the chatter of the conscious mind and tapping into the deeper recesses of our subconscious, we gain access to insights, intuitions, and inspirations that can guide us towards wealth and success.

Furthermore, harnessing the subconscious mind involves the practice of gratitude and appreciation. By expressing gratitude for the abundance that already exists in our lives, we signal to the subconscious that we are open and receptive to receiving more blessings and opportunities.

In essence, harnessing the subconscious mind is about unlocking the hidden potential within us and leveraging it to create wealth and abundance in all areas of our lives. By aligning our thoughts, beliefs, and intentions with our deepest desires, we tap into the limitless power of the subconscious and unleash a torrent of wealth and prosperity.

So, dear reader, I encourage you to explore the practice of harnessing your subconscious mind in your own life. Embrace positive affirmations, visualize your goals, cultivate an abundance mindset, practice mindfulness and meditation, and express gratitude for the blessings in your life. For when you learn to harness the power of your subconscious mind, you unlock the hidden key to wealth and abundance.

Deep within the recesses of our minds lies a reservoir of untapped potential waiting to be unleashed. In this chapter, we delve into the profound influence of the subconscious mind and how harnessing its power can unlock the path to wealth and abundance.

The subconscious mind operates beneath the surface of our conscious awareness, influencing our thoughts, beliefs, and behaviors in subtle yet profound ways. It is the storehouse of our deepest desires, fears, and aspirations, shaping our perceptions of ourselves and the world around us.

One of the key principles of harnessing the power of the subconscious mind is the practice of visualization. By vividly imagining our goals and desires as if they have already been achieved, we imprint them into our subconscious and create a powerful magnet for attracting wealth and abundance into our lives.

Moreover, the subconscious mind is highly receptive to suggestion, making it susceptible to both positive and negative influences. By consciously feeding our minds with thoughts of abundance, prosperity, and success, we can reprogram our subconscious beliefs and remove the mental barriers that may be blocking our path to wealth.

Another aspect of harnessing the power of the subconscious mind is the practice of affirmations. By repeatedly affirming positive statements about ourselves and our ability to achieve wealth and success, we reinforce these beliefs at a subconscious level and create a fertile mental environment for growth and prosperity.

Furthermore, the subconscious mind is a powerful problem-solving tool. By posing questions to our subconscious before we sleep and allowing our minds to work on them overnight, we can tap into its innate wisdom and intuition to find creative solutions to challenges and obstacles that may be hindering our financial success.

In essence, harnessing the power of the subconscious mind is about aligning our thoughts, beliefs, and intentions with our deepest desires and aspirations. By cultivating a positive mental attitude, practicing visualization and affirmation, and tapping into our subconscious wisdom, we can unlock the hidden key to wealth and abundance.

So, dear reader, I encourage you to explore the practice of harnessing your subconscious mind in your own life. Cultivate mindfulness, embrace positive thinking, and unleash the limitless potential that resides within you. For when we learn to harness the power of our subconscious mind, we unlock the door to unlimited wealth and abundance.

HARNESSING THE SUBCONSCIOUS MIND: THE HIDDEN KEY TO WEALTH

13

13

The Role of Autosuggestion: Programming Your Success

Autosuggestion is the art of influencing our subconscious minds through repeated affirmations and suggestions. In this chapter, we explore the pivotal role of autosuggestion in programming our minds for success and unlocking our full potential.

At its core, autosuggestion operates on the principle that our thoughts and beliefs shape our reality. By consciously directing our thoughts towards positive outcomes and affirming our beliefs in our ability to succeed, we can reprogram our subconscious minds and create a mental environment conducive to achievement.

One of the key aspects of autosuggestion is the practice of affirmations. Affirmations are positive statements that we repeat to ourselves regularly, often in the form of "I am" statements. By affirming our goals, strengths, and capabilities, we embed these beliefs into our subconscious minds and cultivate the confidence and self-assurance needed to achieve success.

Moreover, autosuggestion involves the use of visualization techniques to reinforce our affirmations and mental imagery. By vividly imagining ourselves achieving our goals and experiencing the emotions associated with success, we create a powerful mental blueprint that guides our thoughts, actions, and behaviors towards the desired outcome.

THE ROLE OF AUTOSUGGESTION: PROGRAMMING YOUR SUCCESS

Another aspect of autosuggestion is the use of self-talk to reinforce positive beliefs and overcome self-limiting beliefs. By replacing negative self-talk with empowering affirmations and constructive feedback, we can silence our inner critic and cultivate a mindset of abundance and possibility.

Furthermore, autosuggestion can be enhanced through the use of external cues and triggers that reinforce our desired beliefs and behaviors. Whether through visual reminders, affirmations, or surrounding ourselves with supportive individuals, we can create an environment that reinforces our commitment to success and amplifies the impact of our autosuggestions.

In essence, autosuggestion is a powerful tool for reprogramming our minds and shaping our destinies. By harnessing the power of positive affirmations, visualization, and self-talk, we can overcome self-doubt, unlock our full potential, and achieve success in all areas of our lives.

So, dear reader, I encourage you to harness the power of autosuggestion in your own life. Practice affirmations regularly, visualize your success, and cultivate a positive mindset that empowers you to achieve your goals and fulfill your dreams. For when we program our minds for success, we unlock the keys to a life of abundance and fulfillment.

Autosuggestion serves as the bridge between our conscious and subconscious minds, allowing us to program our thoughts and beliefs for success. In this chapter, we explore the profound role of autosuggestion in shaping our destinies and unlocking our fullest potential.

Autosuggestion is the practice of self-directed affirmations and positive statements aimed at influencing our subconscious mind. By repeatedly affirming our desired outcomes and beliefs, we imprint these suggestions into our subconscious, creating a powerful internal dialogue that shapes our perceptions and behaviors.

One of the key principles of autosuggestion is the repetition of positive affirmations. By consistently affirming statements such as "I am capable," "I am deserving of success," and "I attract abundance into my life," we reinforce these beliefs at a subconscious level, paving the way for success and fulfillment.

Moreover, autosuggestion is most effective when paired with vivid imagery and emotion. By visualizing ourselves achieving our goals and experiencing the emotions associated with success, we create a compelling mental image that resonates deeply with our subconscious mind, making it more receptive to our suggestions.

Another aspect of autosuggestion is the importance of belief and expectancy. In order for autosuggestion to be effective, we must wholeheartedly believe in the statements we are affirming and expect them to manifest in our lives. This unwavering faith in the power of autosuggestion strengthens its influence on our subconscious mind and accelerates the realization of our goals.

Furthermore, autosuggestion is a tool for self-empowerment and personal growth. By taking control of our internal dialogue and consciously directing our thoughts and beliefs towards success, we cultivate a mindset of positivity, resilience, and abundance that propels us towards our goals.

In essence, autosuggestion is the process of reprogramming our minds for success. By harnessing the power of positive affirmations, vivid imagery, belief, and expectancy, we can override limiting beliefs and mental barriers, unlocking our full potential and creating the life of our dreams.

So, dear reader, I encourage you to embrace the practice of autosuggestion in your own life. Take control of your internal dialogue, affirm your worth and capabilities, and visualize your success with unwavering belief and expectancy. For when we harness the power of autosuggestion, we program our minds for success and unlock the unlimited potential that resides within us.

THE ROLE OF AUTOSUGGESTION: PROGRAMMING YOUR SUCCESS

14

14

Overcoming Fear: Embracing Courage in Adversity

Fear is a natural part of the human experience, but it need not dictate the course of our lives. In this chapter, we explore the transformative power of courage in overcoming fear and navigating adversity with grace and resilience.

At its core, fear is a primal instinct designed to protect us from perceived threats. However, in today's complex world, fear often manifests as self-doubt, anxiety, and hesitation, holding us back from pursuing our dreams and embracing new opportunities.

The key to overcoming fear lies in cultivating courage - the willingness to confront our fears head-on and take bold action in spite of them. Courage is not the absence of fear, but rather the ability to move forward in the face of it, guided by our convictions and values.

One of the most effective ways to overcome fear is through exposure and desensitization. By gradually exposing ourselves to the object of our fear in a controlled and supportive environment, we can reduce its power over us and build confidence in our ability to cope with adversity.

Moreover, overcoming fear requires a shift in perspective. Instead of seeing fear as a barrier to success, we can choose to view it as a catalyst for growth and transformation. By reframing our fears as opportunities for learning and personal development, we empower ourselves to embrace challenges with courage and resilience.

Another powerful tool for overcoming fear is mindfulness. By bringing awareness to our thoughts and emotions without judgment, we can develop a greater sense of inner peace and equanimity, allowing us to navigate fear with greater clarity and composure.

Furthermore, overcoming fear involves cultivating a strong support network of friends, family, and mentors who can provide encouragement, guidance, and perspective during times of uncertainty and doubt.

In essence, overcoming fear is about stepping out of our comfort zones, embracing vulnerability, and trusting in our ability to handle whatever challenges come our way. By cultivating courage, shifting our perspective, practicing mindfulness, and building a support network, we can conquer our fears and unlock our fullest potential.

So, dear reader, I encourage you to embrace the journey of overcoming fear in your own life. Have the courage to face your fears, knowing that on the other side lies growth, resilience, and a life of purpose and fulfillment.

Fear is a natural and powerful emotion that can often hold us back from reaching our full potential. In this chapter, we explore the transformative journey of overcoming fear and embracing courage in the face of adversity.

Fear has the potential to paralyze us, preventing us from taking risks, pursuing our dreams, and seizing opportunities for growth. It whispers doubt in our ears and fills our minds with worst-case scenarios, keeping us trapped in our comfort zones and preventing us from realizing our true potential.

However, overcoming fear is not about the absence of fear but rather about learning to confront and transcend it. It is about acknowledging our fears, understanding their root causes, and summoning the courage to face them head-on.

One of the key strategies for overcoming fear is reframing our mindset. Instead of viewing fear as a barrier to success, we can choose to see it as an opportunity for growth and self-discovery. By reframing fear as a natural and necessary part of the journey towards our goals, we empower ourselves to confront it with courage and resilience.

Moreover, overcoming fear requires us to cultivate a sense of self-confidence and self-belief. By focusing on our strengths, accomplishments, and past successes, we can bolster our confidence and quiet the voice of doubt that lurks within us.

Another powerful tool for overcoming fear is visualization. By vividly imagining ourselves confronting and overcoming our fears, we desensitize ourselves to them and build the mental resilience needed to face them in real life.

Furthermore, seeking support from others can be instrumental in overcoming fear. By surrounding ourselves with a supportive network of friends, family, and mentors who encourage and uplift us, we gain strength and courage to confront our fears and pursue our goals.

In essence, overcoming fear is a journey of self-discovery and empowerment. By acknowledging our fears, reframing our mindset, cultivating self-confidence, visualizing success, and seeking support from others, we can break free from the shackles of fear and embrace courage in the face of adversity.

So, dear reader, I encourage you to confront your fears head-on, knowing that on the other side lies growth, resilience, and untold possibilities. Embrace courage as your companion on the journey towards your dreams, and watch as fear transforms from a barrier into a stepping stone towards your greatest achievements.

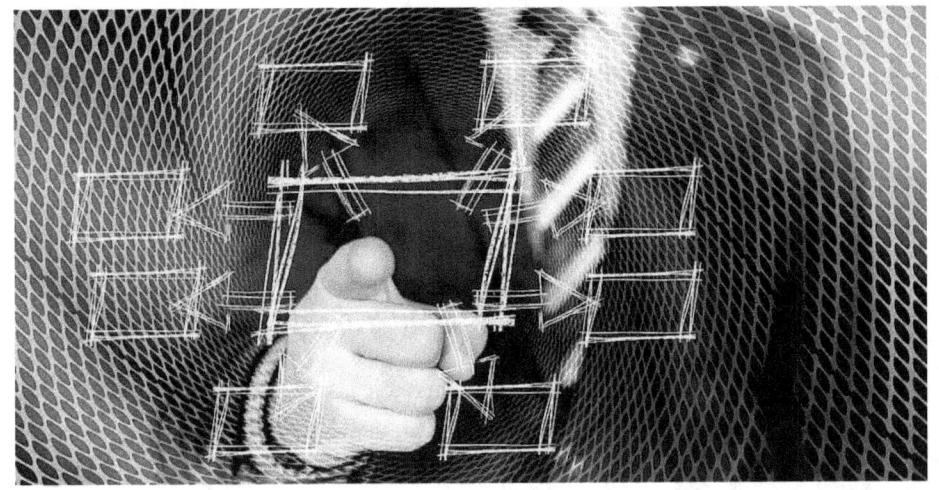

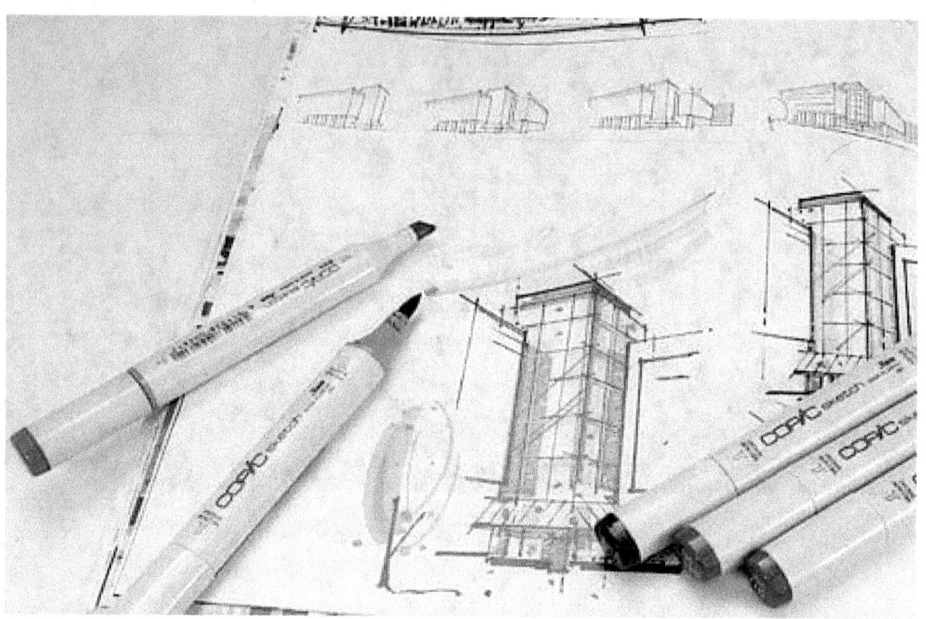

15

15

Building Self-Confidence: The Catalyst for Achievement

Self-confidence is the bedrock upon which our achievements are built, empowering us to embrace challenges, pursue opportunities, and realize our fullest potential. In this chapter, we explore the transformative power of self-confidence and how it serves as the catalyst for success.

At its core, self-confidence is the belief in our own abilities, worth, and potential for success. It is the unwavering conviction that we are capable of overcoming obstacles and achieving our goals, regardless of the challenges we may face along the way.

One of the key elements of building self-confidence is self-awareness. By understanding our strengths, weaknesses, and areas for growth, we can cultivate a realistic and balanced sense of self-assurance that is rooted in our authentic selves.

Moreover, building self-confidence requires us to challenge and reframe negative self-talk and limiting beliefs. Instead of dwelling on our shortcomings and failures, we can choose to focus on our successes and accomplishments, recognizing the progress we have made and the potential for growth that lies within us.

Another important aspect of building self-confidence is setting and achieving goals. By setting clear, achievable objectives and taking consistent action towards their attainment, we build momentum and reinforce our belief in our ability to succeed.

Furthermore, building self-confidence involves stepping outside of our comfort zones and embracing new challenges. By pushing ourselves beyond our perceived limits and experiencing success in unfamiliar territory, we expand our comfort zones and cultivate a sense of resilience and courage that bolsters our confidence.

In essence, building self-confidence is a journey of self-discovery and personal growth. By cultivating self-awareness, challenging negative self-talk, setting and achieving goals, and embracing new challenges, we can unlock the limitless potential that lies within us and achieve our greatest aspirations.

So, dear reader, I encourage you to embrace the journey of building self-confidence in your own life. Believe in yourself, celebrate your strengths, and take bold action towards your goals with unwavering conviction and determination. For when you cultivate self-confidence as the catalyst for achievement, you unlock the door to endless possibilities and pave the way for a life of fulfillment and success.

Self-confidence is the cornerstone upon which our achievements are built, empowering us to pursue our goals with determination and resilience. In this chapter, we delve into the transformative power of building self-confidence and its role as the catalyst for success.

Self-confidence is more than just a belief in our abilities; it is a deep-seated trust in ourselves and our capacity to overcome challenges and achieve our aspirations. It is the foundation of a positive self-image and a resilient mindset that propels us forward in the face of adversity.

One of the key strategies for building self-confidence is setting and achieving small goals. By breaking our larger aspirations into manageable steps and celebrating our progress along the way, we build momentum and cultivate a sense of accomplishment that bolsters our confidence.

Moreover, building self-confidence involves challenging our inner critic and reframing negative self-talk. Instead of dwelling on our shortcomings and failures, we can choose to focus on our strengths, accomplishments, and past successes, fostering a more positive and empowering internal dialogue.

Another powerful tool for building self-confidence is the practice of visualization. By vividly imagining ourselves achieving our goals and experiencing the feelings of success, we program our subconscious minds for achievement and create a mental blueprint for realizing our aspirations.

Furthermore, surrounding ourselves with supportive and encouraging individuals can be instrumental in building self-confidence. By seeking out mentors, friends, and allies who believe in our potential and cheer us on, we gain the courage and resilience needed to pursue our goals with conviction.

In essence, building self-confidence is a journey of self-discovery and self-empowerment. By setting and achieving goals, challenging negative self-talk, practicing visualization, and surrounding ourselves with supportive allies, we cultivate the unshakable belief in ourselves that is the foundation of success.

So, dear reader, I encourage you to embrace the practice of building self-confidence in your own life. Trust in your abilities, celebrate your successes, and face your challenges with courage and resilience. For when you believe in yourself, anything is possible, and the world becomes your oyster.

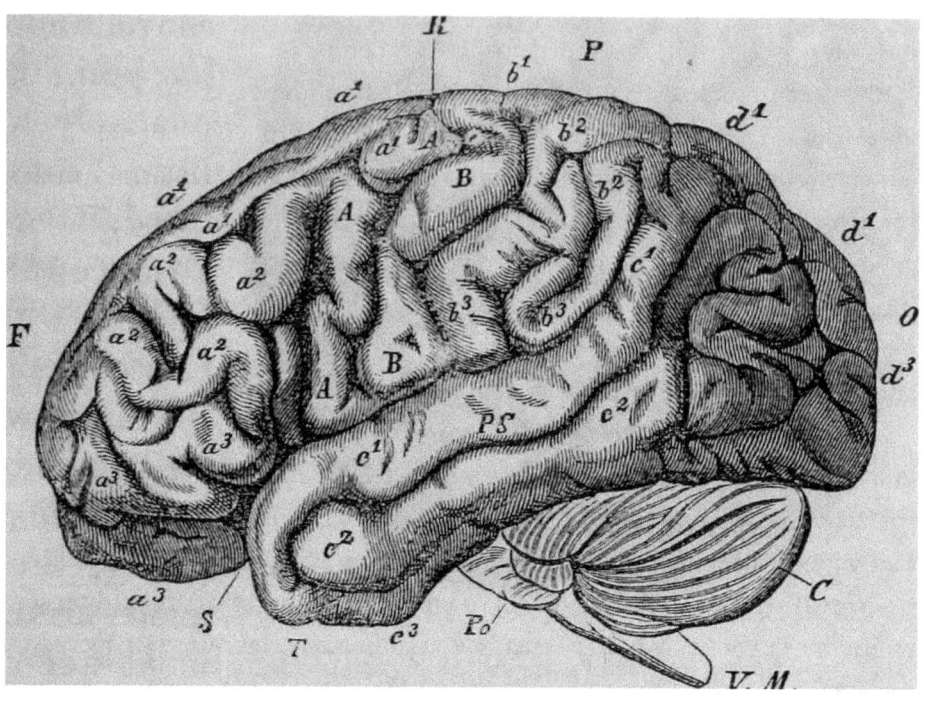

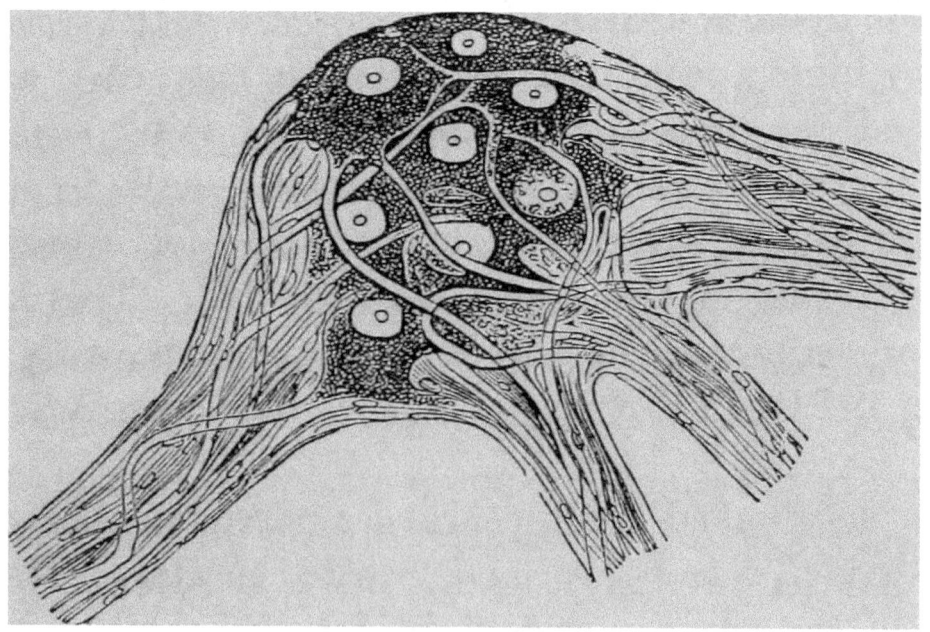

16

16

The Power of Imagination: Crafting Your Ideal Future

Imagination is the canvas upon which we paint the masterpiece of our lives, shaping our reality and paving the way to our ideal future. In this chapter, we explore the transformative power of imagination and its role in crafting the life we desire.

At its essence, imagination is the ability to conceive of possibilities beyond our current circumstances, to envision a reality that has yet to be realized. It is the fuel that ignites our creativity, drives innovation, and propels us toward our goals.

One of the key principles of harnessing the power of imagination is the practice of visualization. By vividly imagining ourselves living the life of our dreams - experiencing success, abundance, and fulfillment - we create a mental blueprint that guides our actions and shapes our reality.

Moreover, imagination is a potent tool for problem-solving and innovation. By allowing our minds to wander freely and explore new ideas and possibilities, we can uncover innovative solutions to challenges and obstacles that may be hindering our progress.

Another aspect of the power of imagination is its ability to inspire and motivate us to take action. When we can clearly envision our desired future and the steps needed to achieve it, we are more likely to take proactive steps toward realizing our goals.

Furthermore, imagination is a source of boundless creativity and inspiration. By tapping into our imagination, we can unleash our innate creativity and discover new ways of thinking, being, and doing that can lead to breakthroughs and transformation in our lives.

In essence, the power of imagination is the key to unlocking our limitless potential and creating the life we desire. By harnessing the power of visualization, fostering creativity and innovation, and allowing ourselves to dream big, we can craft a future that surpasses our wildest dreams.

So, dear reader, I encourage you to embrace the power of imagination in your own life. Dare to dream, envision your ideal future, and take inspired action to bring it into reality. For when you harness the power of your imagination, the possibilities are endless, and the world becomes your playground for creation and exploration.

Imagination is the canvas upon which we paint the vivid tapestry of our lives, shaping our dreams into reality and charting the course to our ideal future. In this chapter, we explore the transformative potential of imagination and its role in manifesting our deepest desires.

At its essence, imagination is the ability to envision possibilities beyond the constraints of our current reality. It is the creative force that sparks innovation, inspires invention, and fuels our aspirations. Through the power of imagination, we can transcend limitations and dare to dream of a future filled with possibility and abundance.

One of the key aspects of harnessing the power of imagination is the practice of visualization. By vividly imagining our goals and desires as if they have already been achieved, we create a mental blueprint that aligns our thoughts, emotions, and actions with our desired outcomes. Visualization activates the subconscious mind, programming it to seek out opportunities and solutions that lead us closer to our dreams.

Moreover, imagination is a tool for problem-solving and innovation. By exploring alternative scenarios and envisioning creative solutions to challenges, we tap into the boundless wellspring of our imagination to overcome obstacles and forge new pathways to success.

THE POWER OF IMAGINATION: CRAFTING YOUR IDEAL FUTURE

Another aspect of the power of imagination is its ability to inspire and motivate us towards action. When we envision our ideal future with clarity and passion, we ignite a fire within us that drives us to take bold and decisive steps towards its realization. Imagination fuels our ambition, propelling us forward even in the face of uncertainty and adversity.

Furthermore, imagination fosters a sense of possibility and optimism that fuels our resilience and perseverance in the face of setbacks. By cultivating a mindset of abundance and possibility, we can transform obstacles into opportunities and setbacks into stepping stones towards our goals.

In essence, the power of imagination is the key to crafting our ideal future. By harnessing its creative force, we can envision the life we desire and manifest it into reality. So, dear reader, I encourage you to unleash the power of your imagination, dare to dream big, and embark on the journey of transforming your dreams into reality.

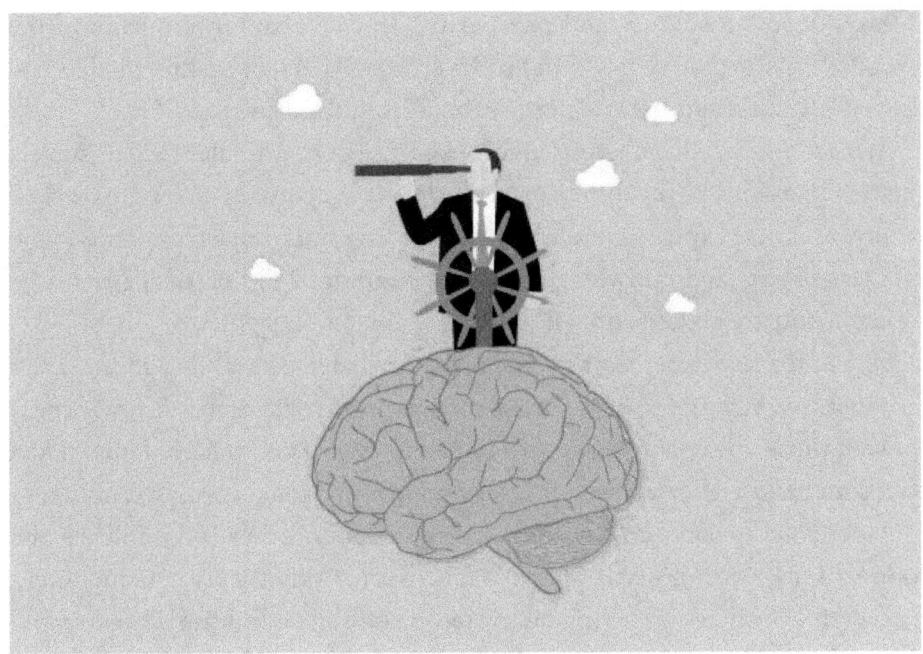

17

17

Using Specialized Knowledge: The Currency of Experts

Specialized knowledge is the currency of experts, the key that unlocks doors to success and prosperity. In this chapter, we explore the transformative potential of leveraging specialized knowledge and how it distinguishes the truly exceptional from the average.

At its core, specialized knowledge is expertise in a particular field or subject matter that goes beyond the surface level. It is acquired through years of study, practical experience, and a relentless pursuit of mastery. Those who possess specialized knowledge have a deep understanding of their chosen domain and are able to apply it with precision and insight.

One of the key benefits of specialized knowledge is its ability to provide a competitive advantage in the marketplace. In a world where knowledge is power, those who possess expertise in a niche area are in high demand and can command higher salaries, greater opportunities, and increased influence.

Moreover, specialized knowledge opens doors to new possibilities and opportunities for growth and advancement. Whether it's launching a successful business, securing a coveted position, or making a meaningful impact in your field, specialized knowledge gives you the edge you need to stand out and succeed.

Another aspect of leveraging specialized knowledge is its potential for innovation and creativity. By deeply understanding the intricacies of a particular field, you are better equipped to identify gaps, solve complex problems, and develop groundbreaking solutions that push the boundaries of what is possible.

Furthermore, specialized knowledge allows you to build credibility and authority within your industry. By consistently delivering high-quality work and demonstrating your expertise, you establish yourself as a trusted advisor and thought leader, earning the respect and admiration of your peers and colleagues.

In essence, specialized knowledge is the currency of experts, the key that unlocks doors to success and prosperity. By investing in your education, honing your skills, and continuously expanding your knowledge base, you position yourself for greatness and open yourself up to a world of endless possibilities.

So, dear reader, I encourage you to embrace the power of specialized knowledge in your own life. Identify your areas of interest and passion, commit yourself to lifelong learning, and become a true master of your craft. For when you harness the transformative potential of specialized knowledge, the sky's the limit for what you can achieve.

Specialized knowledge is the currency of experts, the key that unlocks doors to success and distinction. In this chapter, we delve into the significance of specialized knowledge and how leveraging it can propel us to new heights of achievement and recognition.

At its core, specialized knowledge is the result of focused study, experience, and expertise in a particular field or subject matter. It represents a deep understanding of specialized topics, techniques, and insights that set individuals apart as authorities and thought leaders in their respective fields.

One of the key benefits of specialized knowledge is its ability to provide a competitive edge in today's rapidly evolving and competitive marketplace. By becoming experts in our chosen fields, we position ourselves as valuable assets to employers, clients, and collaborators, opening doors to new opportunities and advancement.

Moreover, specialized knowledge enables us to solve complex problems and address specific challenges with precision and efficiency. By honing our expertise in a particular area, we gain the insights and capabilities needed to navigate complexities, innovate solutions, and deliver exceptional results.

Another aspect of specialized knowledge is its capacity to foster credibility and authority within our industries and communities. As experts in our fields, we earn the trust and respect of our peers, clients, and audiences, establishing ourselves as trusted advisors and influencers whose opinions carry weight and influence.

Furthermore, specialized knowledge provides a pathway to personal and professional growth and fulfillment. By continuously expanding our expertise and staying abreast of developments in our fields, we remain at the forefront of innovation and progress, enriching our lives and contributing to the greater good.

In essence, specialized knowledge is the currency of experts, the fuel that drives innovation, excellence, and distinction in every field of endeavor. By leveraging our expertise and sharing our insights with others, we contribute to the collective advancement of knowledge and human achievement.

So, dear reader, I encourage you to embrace the pursuit of specialized knowledge in your own life. Invest in your education, cultivate your expertise, and strive to become a recognized authority in your chosen field. For when you harness the power of specialized knowledge, you unlock the door to limitless possibilities and opportunities for success and fulfillment.

USING SPECIALIZED KNOWLEDGE: THE CURRENCY OF EXPERTS

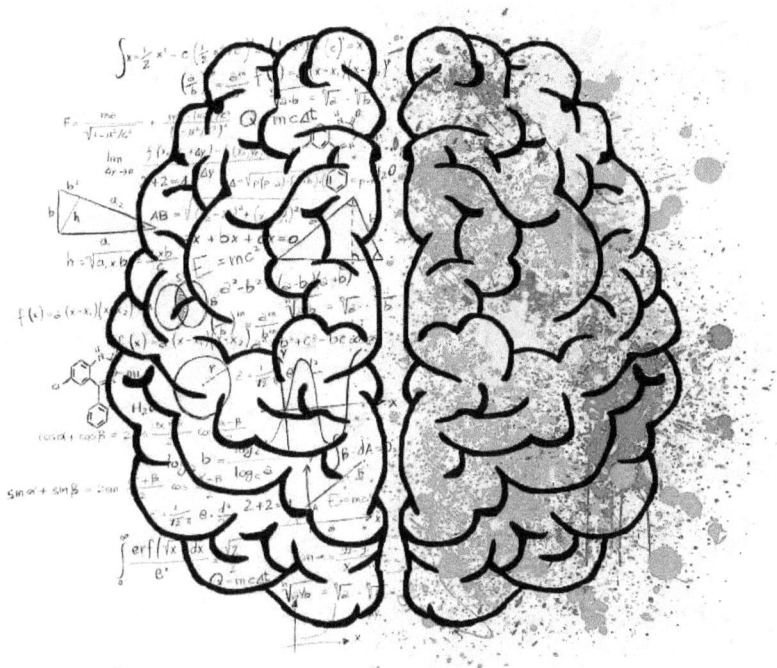

18

18

Tapping into the Infinite Intelligence: Connecting with Universal Wisdom

Within the vast expanse of the universe lies a boundless wellspring of wisdom and insight, waiting to be tapped into by those who seek to expand their understanding and consciousness. In this chapter, we explore the transformative journey of connecting with universal wisdom and harnessing the power of infinite intelligence.

At the heart of tapping into infinite intelligence lies the recognition that we are part of a greater whole, interconnected with all living beings and the universe itself. By quieting the noise of the mind and opening ourselves up to the flow of universal energy, we can access profound insights and guidance that transcend individual knowledge and experience.

One of the key practices for tapping into infinite intelligence is meditation. Through the practice of meditation, we create space for silence and stillness, allowing us to quiet the chatter of the mind and tune into the deeper currents of universal wisdom that flow within and around us.

Moreover, tapping into infinite intelligence involves cultivating a mindset of openness and receptivity to new ideas and perspectives. By releasing attachment to preconceived notions and embracing a sense of curiosity and wonder, we invite new insights and revelations to emerge into our awareness.

Another aspect of tapping into infinite intelligence is the practice of mindfulness. By cultivating present moment awareness and paying attention to the subtle cues and synchronicities that unfold in our lives, we can discern the guiding hand of universal intelligence at work, leading us towards greater clarity and alignment with our true purpose.

Furthermore, tapping into infinite intelligence involves trusting our intuition and inner guidance. By quieting the rational mind and listening to the whispers of our hearts, we can access the intuitive wisdom that resides within us, guiding us towards decisions and actions that are in alignment with our highest good.

In essence, tapping into infinite intelligence is a journey of self-discovery and spiritual awakening. By quieting the mind, opening the heart, and trusting the wisdom of the universe, we can access profound insights and guidance that illuminate our path and empower us to live lives of purpose, passion, and fulfillment.

So, dear reader, I encourage you to embark on the journey of tapping into infinite intelligence in your own life. Cultivate practices such as meditation, mindfulness, and intuition, and open yourself up to the flow of universal wisdom that surrounds you. For when you connect with infinite intelligence, you align yourself with the greater purpose and meaning of life, and unlock the door to boundless possibilities and potential.

Within the vast expanse of the universe lies an infinite wellspring of wisdom waiting to be tapped into. In this chapter, we explore the profound journey of connecting with universal intelligence and harnessing its boundless insights to navigate life's challenges and unlock our fullest potential.

At the heart of tapping into infinite intelligence is the recognition that we are interconnected with the cosmos and imbued with the same creative energy that shapes the universe. By quieting our minds and opening our hearts to the wisdom that surrounds us, we can access a deeper understanding of ourselves and the world around us.

One of the key practices for connecting with universal wisdom is meditation. By quieting the chatter of our minds and tuning into the stillness within, we create space for intuitive insights and divine inspiration to flow freely. Through regular meditation practice, we can cultivate a deeper connection with our inner wisdom and the universal intelligence that animates all of creation.

Moreover, connecting with infinite intelligence involves embracing a mindset of openness and receptivity to new ideas and perspectives. By remaining curious, humble, and open-minded, we create space for growth and transformation, allowing the universe to reveal its secrets to us in unexpected and profound ways.

Another aspect of tapping into universal wisdom is the practice of mindfulness. By cultivating present moment awareness and paying attention to the signs and synchronicities that present themselves in our lives, we can discern the guidance and wisdom that the universe is constantly offering us.

Furthermore, connecting with infinite intelligence involves trusting in the inherent wisdom of the universe and surrendering to the flow of life. By relinquishing the need for control and allowing ourselves to be guided by divine intelligence, we can navigate life's twists and turns with grace and ease.

In essence, tapping into the infinite intelligence is a journey of self-discovery, spiritual growth, and profound connection with the cosmos. By cultivating practices such as meditation, mindfulness, openness, and surrender, we can access the timeless wisdom that lies at the heart of existence and unlock our fullest potential.

So, dear reader, I encourage you to embark on the journey of connecting with universal wisdom in your own life. Trust in the guidance of the universe, listen to the whispers of your soul, and open yourself up to the infinite possibilities that await you. For when you tap into the boundless intelligence of the cosmos, you align yourself with the flow of life and unlock the secrets of the universe.

19

19

The Power of the Master Mind Alliance: Synergizing with Like-Minded Individuals

The Master Mind Alliance is a powerhouse of collective energy, where minds converge, ideas flourish, and greatness is born. In this chapter, we explore the profound impact of forming alliances with like-minded individuals and how synergy can propel us towards unprecedented levels of success and fulfillment.

At its essence, the Master Mind Alliance is a synergistic collaboration of individuals who come together with a shared purpose, vision, and commitment to supporting each other's growth and success. It is a sacred space where ideas are shared, challenges are overcome, and dreams are transformed into reality through the collective power of minds working in harmony.

One of the key benefits of the Master Mind Alliance is the diversity of perspectives and expertise that its members bring to the table. By collaborating with individuals from different backgrounds, industries, and areas of expertise, we gain access to a wealth of knowledge, insights, and experiences that enrich our own understanding and broaden our horizons.

Moreover, the Master Mind Alliance provides a supportive environment where members can hold each other accountable, provide constructive feedback, and offer encouragement and support. It is a place where vulnerabilities are shared, challenges are met with empathy, and victories are celebrated with genuine enthusiasm.

Another aspect of the power of the Master Mind Alliance is its ability to foster creativity and innovation through the exchange of ideas and brainstorming sessions. By bouncing ideas off each other and engaging in collaborative problem-solving, members can uncover new perspectives, identify innovative solutions, and push the boundaries of what is possible.

Furthermore, the Master Mind Alliance serves as a catalyst for personal and professional growth and development. By surrounding ourselves with high-achieving individuals who inspire and challenge us to be our best selves, we elevate our standards, expand our capabilities, and accelerate our progress towards our goals.

In essence, the power of the Master Mind Alliance lies in its ability to amplify our individual strengths, overcome our collective weaknesses, and achieve more together than we ever could alone. By harnessing the collective wisdom, energy, and resources of like-minded individuals, we unlock the door to unlimited possibilities and opportunities for growth and success.

So, dear reader, I encourage you to seek out opportunities to form alliances with like-minded individuals who share your vision and values. Surround yourself with a supportive network of peers, mentors, and collaborators who challenge and inspire you to reach new heights of achievement and fulfillment. For when you harness the power of the Master Mind Alliance, you tap into a reservoir of collective energy and wisdom that can propel you towards your greatest aspirations.

In the realm of achievement, the collective power of minds united towards a common purpose is unparalleled. In this chapter, we delve into the transformative potential of the Master Mind Alliance and the extraordinary synergy that emerges when like-minded individuals come together.

The Master Mind Alliance is a collective of individuals who share a common vision, values, and goals, pooling their talents, resources, and insights to support one another's aspirations. It is a dynamic force for collaboration, innovation, and mutual growth that transcends the limitations of individual effort.

One of the key benefits of the Master Mind Alliance is the opportunity for collaborative learning and brainstorming. By engaging in open dialogue and exchanging ideas with others who share our passions and ambitions, we gain fresh perspectives, insights, and solutions that can inspire breakthroughs and accelerate our progress.

Moreover, the Master Mind Alliance fosters a supportive environment where members challenge and encourage one another to reach new heights of achievement. The collective wisdom and encouragement of the group provide a source of motivation, accountability, and inspiration that fuels our determination and resilience in the face of challenges.

Another aspect of the Master Mind Alliance is the opportunity for networking and collaboration. By connecting with individuals from diverse backgrounds and industries, we expand our professional network and open doors to new opportunities for collaboration, partnership, and growth.

Furthermore, the Master Mind Alliance serves as a catalyst for personal and professional development. Through shared experiences, feedback, and mentorship, members of the group can overcome limiting beliefs, develop new skills, and unlock their fullest potential.

In essence, the Master Mind Alliance is a powerful vehicle for collective achievement and personal transformation. By synergizing with like-minded individuals who share our vision and values, we amplify our impact, expand our possibilities, and achieve greater levels of success than we could ever imagine on our own.

So, dear reader, I encourage you to seek out or create your own MasterMind Alliance in your own life. Surround yourself with individuals who share your passions, aspirations, and values, and harness the extraordinary power of collective intelligence, collaboration, and support. For when minds unite in harmony, miracles happen, and the impossible becomes possible.

20

20

Taking Inspired Action: Seizing Opportunities

Opportunities are the seeds of greatness, but it is action that nourishes their growth. In this chapter, we explore the transformative power of taking inspired action and seizing the opportunities that come our way.

Inspired action is the deliberate choice to act in alignment with our deepest desires, passions, and values. It is the fuel that propels us forward on the path to our dreams, transforming potential into reality and vision into manifestation.

One of the key aspects of taking inspired action is cultivating a mindset of openness and receptivity to new possibilities. By remaining curious, adventurous, and open-minded, we create space for serendipity and synchronicity to guide us towards unexpected opportunities and experiences.

Moreover, taking inspired action involves trusting our intuition and inner guidance to lead us towards our highest good. By tuning into the wisdom of our hearts and souls, we can discern the opportunities that resonate with our deepest desires and aspirations, and take decisive steps to pursue them.

Another aspect of taking inspired action is embracing the courage to step outside our comfort zones and embrace the unknown. Growth and transformation often lie on the other side of fear, and it is through taking bold and courageous action that we expand our horizons and unlock new levels of potential.

Furthermore, taking inspired action requires us to be proactive and resourceful in seeking out opportunities for growth and advancement. Rather than waiting for opportunities to come to us, we actively seek them out, network with others, and create our own pathways to success.

In essence, taking inspired action is about embodying the spirit of initiative, creativity, and determination in pursuit of our goals and aspirations. By seizing the opportunities that come our way and taking decisive action to bring our dreams to fruition, we align ourselves with the flow of life and unlock the limitless possibilities that await us.

So, dear reader, I encourage you to embrace the practice of taking inspired action in your own life. Trust in your intuition, step outside your comfort zone, and seize the opportunities that come your way with courage and conviction. For when you take inspired action, you harness the power to create the life of your dreams and fulfill your greatest potential.

Opportunities are the doorways to our dreams, waiting for us to take inspired action and turn them into reality. In this chapter, we explore the transformative power of taking inspired action and seizing the opportunities that come our way.

Inspired action is the act of moving forward with purpose, passion, and determination, fueled by the vision of our goals and aspirations. It is the willingness to step outside our comfort zones, take risks, and pursue our dreams with unwavering commitment and enthusiasm.

One of the key principles of taking inspired action is the ability to recognize and seize opportunities as they arise. Opportunities are often disguised as challenges or setbacks, requiring us to approach them with an open mind and a willingness to explore new possibilities. By staying alert and attuned to the signals and synchronicities that present themselves in our lives, we can recognize opportunities when they appear and take decisive action to capitalize on them.

Moreover, taking inspired action involves trusting our intuition and following our inner guidance. Our intuition is a powerful compass that can lead us towards opportunities and experiences that align with our deepest desires and highest purpose. By tuning into our inner wisdom and listening to the whispers of our soul, we can discern the right course of action and move forward with confidence and clarity.

Another aspect of taking inspired action is the willingness to take calculated risks and embrace uncertainty. While stepping into the unknown can be daunting, it is often where the greatest opportunities for growth and success lie. By embracing uncertainty and trusting in our ability to navigate challenges, we can overcome fear and hesitation and seize the opportunities that lead us towards our goals.

Furthermore, taking inspired action requires perseverance and resilience in the face of obstacles and setbacks. Not every opportunity will lead to immediate success, and there may be times when we encounter setbacks or failures along the way. However, by remaining steadfast in our commitment to our goals and staying resilient in the face of adversity, we can overcome obstacles and continue moving forward towards our dreams.

In essence, taking inspired action is about aligning our thoughts, beliefs, and intentions with our deepest desires and aspirations, and then taking decisive steps towards their realization. It is about embracing opportunities, trusting our intuition, taking calculated risks, and persevering in the face of challenges. When we take inspired action, we open ourselves up to a world of limitless possibilities and potential, and we become the architects of our own destiny.

So, dear reader, I encourage you to embrace the practice of taking inspired action in your own life. Stay open to opportunities, trust in your intuition, and take bold steps towards your dreams. For when you take inspired action, you align yourself with the flow of life, and miracles happen.

21

21

Developing Leadership Skills: Guiding Your Path to Success

Leadership is not merely a title; it is a set of skills and qualities that empower individuals to guide themselves and others towards success. In this chapter, we explore the transformative journey of developing leadership skills and how they can shape our paths to success.

At its essence, leadership is about inspiring and empowering others to achieve their fullest potential. It is about setting a vision, communicating it effectively, and mobilizing people towards common goals. Developing leadership skills is essential not only for those in formal leadership roles but for anyone who seeks to make a positive impact and drive change in their personal and professional lives.

One of the key qualities of effective leadership is self-awareness. Leaders who possess self-awareness understand their strengths, weaknesses, and values, and they are able to lead authentically from a place of integrity and authenticity. By cultivating self-awareness, we can develop a deeper understanding of ourselves and others, and we can lead with empathy, compassion, and humility.

Moreover, effective leadership involves effective communication. Leaders must be able to articulate their vision, listen actively to the perspectives of others, and provide clear and constructive feedback. By honing our communication skills, we can build trust, foster collaboration, and inspire others to action.

Another essential aspect of leadership is the ability to make sound decisions under pressure. Leaders must be able to analyze complex situations, weigh the pros and cons of different courses of action, and make decisions that align with their vision and values. By developing critical thinking and problem-solving skills, we can navigate challenges and obstacles with confidence and clarity.

Furthermore, effective leaders are adept at building and nurturing relationships. They understand the importance of teamwork, collaboration, and emotional intelligence in achieving collective goals. By fostering a culture of trust, respect, and accountability, leaders can create environments where individuals feel valued, empowered, and motivated to contribute their best.

In essence, developing leadership skills is a journey of self-discovery, growth, and continuous learning. By cultivating self-awareness, honing communication skills, making sound decisions, and building relationships, we can unlock our potential as leaders and guide ourselves and others towards success.

So, dear reader, I encourage you to embrace the journey of developing leadership skills in your own life. Take ownership of your growth, seek out opportunities for learning and development, and lead with courage, compassion, and integrity. For when you develop your leadership skills, you empower yourself to make a positive impact and create a legacy of success that inspires others to greatness.

Leadership is not merely a title but a set of skills and qualities that empower individuals to inspire, motivate, and guide others towards shared goals and visions. In this chapter, we explore the transformative journey of developing leadership skills and how they pave the way to success.

At its core, leadership is about influence - the ability to inspire others to willingly follow and collaborate towards a common purpose. Developing leadership skills involves cultivating a range of competencies and qualities that enable individuals to effectively lead and empower others.

One of the key components of developing leadership skills is self-awareness.

DEVELOPING LEADERSHIP SKILLS: GUIDING YOUR PATH TO SUCCESS

Effective leaders have a deep understanding of their strengths, weaknesses, values, and goals. By cultivating self-awareness, individuals can leverage their strengths, address their weaknesses, and align their actions with their values, becoming authentic and inspiring leaders in the process.

Moreover, developing leadership skills requires the ability to communicate effectively and build relationships based on trust, respect, and empathy. Effective leaders are skilled communicators who can articulate their vision, listen actively to others, and provide feedback and support that inspires confidence and commitment in their teams.

Another aspect of developing leadership skills is the ability to inspire and motivate others towards a shared vision. Effective leaders lead by example, embodying the values and principles they espouse and inspiring others to strive for excellence. By fostering a culture of collaboration, innovation, and empowerment, leaders create environments where individuals feel valued, motivated, and inspired to contribute their best.

Furthermore, developing leadership skills involves the capacity to make sound decisions and navigate complexity and uncertainty with confidence and clarity. Effective leaders are strategic thinkers who can analyze situations, weigh options, and make informed decisions that align with their vision and goals. By demonstrating resilience, adaptability, and problem-solving skills, leaders inspire confidence and trust in their teams, even in challenging times.

In essence, developing leadership skills is a journey of continuous learning, growth, and self-discovery. By cultivating self-awareness, effective communication, inspirational leadership, and strategic decision-making, individuals can become the visionary leaders who inspire others and drive success.

So, dear reader, I encourage you to embark on the journey of developing leadership skills in your own life. Cultivate self-awareness, hone your communication skills, inspire others with your vision, and lead with integrity and purpose. For when you develop leadership skills, you not only guide your own path to success but also empower others to reach their fullest potential.

THE POWER

DEVELOPING LEADERSHIP SKILLS: GUIDING YOUR PATH TO SUCCESS

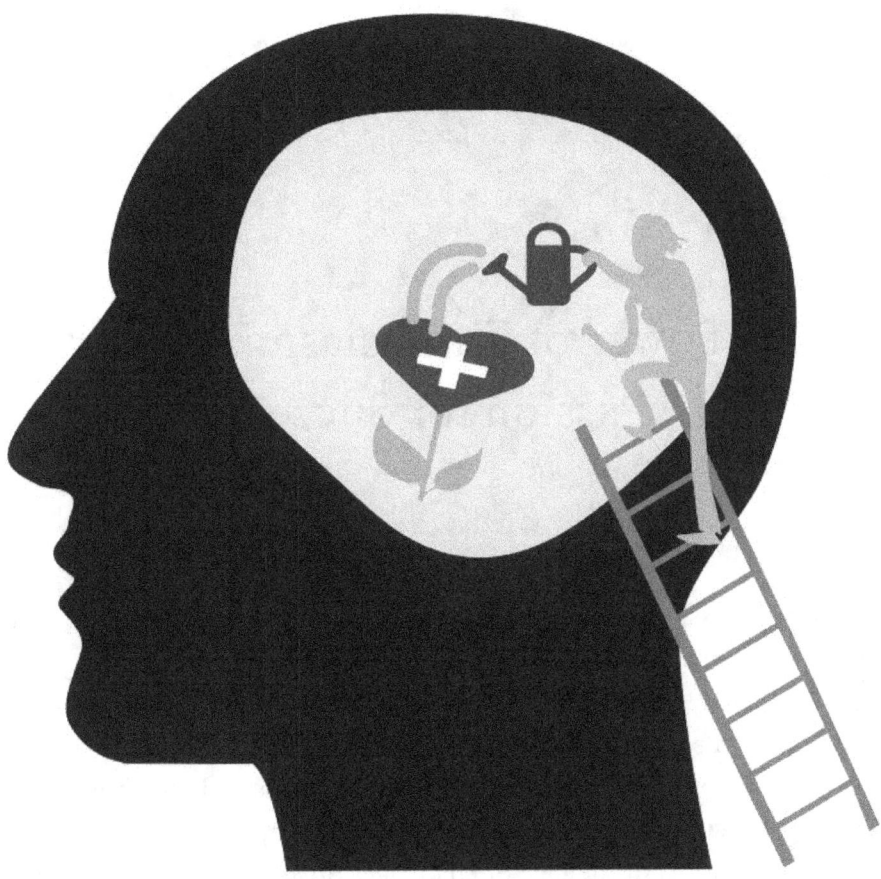

22

The Power of Enthusiasm: Igniting Passion for Success

Enthusiasm is the spark that ignites the flames of passion and drives us towards our goals with unwavering determination. In this chapter, we delve into the transformative power of enthusiasm and its profound impact on achieving success.

At its core, enthusiasm is a contagious energy that radiates from within, infusing our actions with excitement, joy, and purpose. It is the fuel that propels us forward in the face of challenges, inspires others to join us on our journey, and transforms obstacles into opportunities for growth and achievement.

One of the key benefits of enthusiasm is its ability to inspire and motivate both ourselves and those around us. When we approach our goals with enthusiasm and passion, we create a magnetic energy that attracts support, resources, and opportunities into our lives. Others are drawn to our passion and commitment, eager to join us in our endeavors and contribute their talents and support towards our shared vision.

Moreover, enthusiasm is a powerful antidote to doubt, fear, and negativity. When we approach challenges with enthusiasm and optimism, we shift our perspective from focusing on obstacles to embracing possibilities. Enthusiasm empowers us to see setbacks as temporary setbacks and failures as opportunities for growth and learning, fueling our resilience and determination to persevere in the pursuit of our goals.

Another aspect of the power of enthusiasm is its ability to enhance our creativity and innovation. When we approach our work with enthusiasm and passion, we tap into a wellspring of inspiration and intuition that fuels our imagination and ingenuity. Enthusiasm enables us to think outside the box, explore new ideas and possibilities, and find innovative solutions to complex problems.

Furthermore, enthusiasm is a key driver of personal and professional satisfaction and fulfillment. When we engage in activities that ignite our passion and enthusiasm, we experience a deep sense of purpose and fulfillment that transcends material success. Enthusiasm enables us to fully immerse ourselves in our pursuits, savoring the journey and celebrating each milestone along the way.

In essence, the power of enthusiasm is the secret ingredient that transforms dreams into reality and ordinary efforts into extraordinary achievements. By cultivating enthusiasm in our lives and endeavors, we unlock the full potential of our talents and abilities, inspire others to join us on our journey, and create a legacy of passion, purpose, and success.

So, dear reader, I encourage you to embrace the power of enthusiasm in your own life. Cultivate your passions, pursue your goals with zeal and excitement, and let your enthusiasm be the guiding force that propels you towards success and fulfillment. For when you approach life with enthusiasm, the possibilities are endless, and the journey becomes a joyful adventure filled with excitement, discovery, and growth.

Enthusiasm is the spark that ignites our passions, fuels our ambitions, and propels us towards success with unwavering energy and determination. In this chapter, we explore the transformative force of enthusiasm and its profound impact on our journey towards achieving our goals.

At its core, enthusiasm is a contagious energy that radiates from within, infusing every aspect of our lives with vitality, joy, and purpose. It is the fuel that drives us to pursue our dreams with passion and commitment, regardless of the obstacles we may encounter along the way.

One of the key attributes of enthusiasm is its ability to inspire and motivate others. When we approach our goals with enthusiasm and zest, we inspire those around us to believe in themselves and strive for greatness. Enthusiasm is a magnet that attracts like-minded individuals, forming a supportive network of allies and collaborators who share our vision and passion for success.

Moreover, enthusiasm is a catalyst for creativity and innovation. When we are passionate about our pursuits, we approach challenges with a sense of curiosity and openness, leading to new ideas, solutions, and breakthroughs. Enthusiasm fuels our creativity, empowering us to think outside the box and push the boundaries of what is possible.

Another aspect of the power of enthusiasm is its ability to overcome obstacles and setbacks. When we are enthusiastic about our goals, we approach challenges with a positive attitude and unwavering determination, refusing to be deterred by setbacks or failures. Enthusiasm gives us the resilience and perseverance to bounce back from adversity and keep moving forward towards our dreams.

Furthermore, enthusiasm is a source of personal fulfillment and satisfaction. When we pursue our goals with passion and enthusiasm, we experience a sense of purpose and joy that transcends external rewards or recognition. Enthusiasm allows us to fully immerse ourselves in the present moment, savoring the journey as much as the destination.

In essence, the power of enthusiasm lies in its ability to transform our lives and the lives of those around us. By embracing enthusiasm as a guiding force in our pursuit of success, we infuse every aspect of our lives with passion, purpose, and vitality.

So, dear reader, I encourage you to harness the power of enthusiasm in your own life. Approach your goals with passion and zest, inspire others with your energy and commitment, and embrace the journey with joy and enthusiasm. For when you ignite the spark of enthusiasm within yourself, you unlock the door to unlimited possibilities and potential for success.

THE POWER OF ENTHUSIASM: IGNITING PASSION FOR SUCCESS

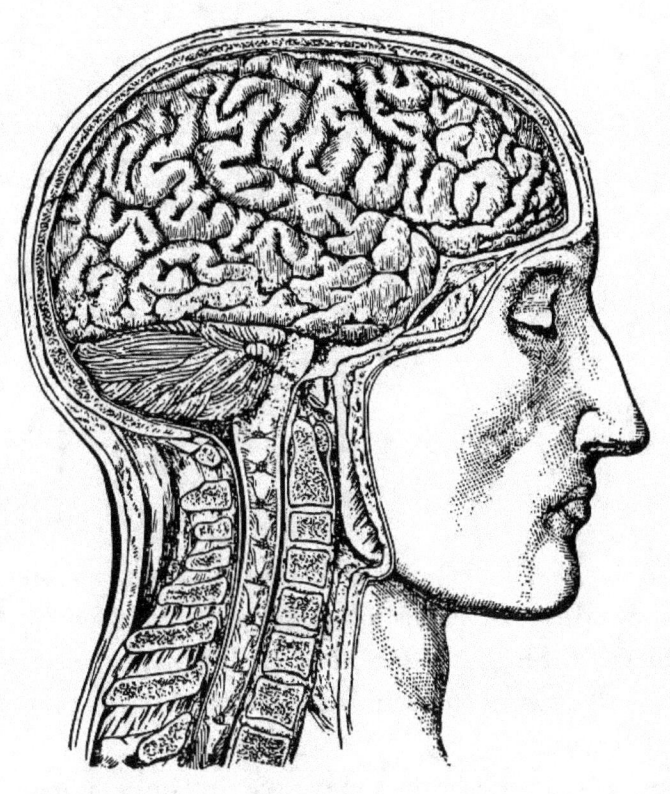

23

23

Cultivating Self-Discipline: The Key to Mastery

Self-discipline is the cornerstone upon which mastery is built, empowering individuals to stay focused, overcome obstacles, and achieve their highest aspirations. In this chapter, we delve into the transformative journey of cultivating self-discipline and its profound impact on our path to mastery.

At its core, self-discipline is the ability to control one's impulses, emotions, and actions in pursuit of long-term goals and aspirations. It requires a commitment to self-control, perseverance, and consistency in the face of distractions, temptations, and setbacks.

One of the key components of cultivating self-discipline is setting clear goals and priorities. By defining our objectives and establishing a roadmap for success, we provide ourselves with a clear sense of direction and purpose, making it easier to stay focused and disciplined in the pursuit of our goals.

Moreover, cultivating self-discipline involves developing healthy habits and routines that support our goals and aspirations. By creating daily rituals and routines that reinforce positive behaviors and eliminate distractions, we set ourselves up for success and make it easier to maintain our focus and momentum over time.

Another aspect of cultivating self-discipline is the ability to manage our time effectively. Time is a finite resource, and how we choose to allocate it can have a significant impact on our ability to achieve our goals. By prioritizing tasks, setting deadlines, and avoiding procrastination, we can make the most of our time and maximize our productivity.

Furthermore, cultivating self-discipline requires resilience and perseverance in the face of challenges and setbacks. There will inevitably be obstacles and setbacks along the journey to mastery, but it is our ability to stay disciplined and focused in the face of adversity that ultimately determines our success.

In essence, cultivating self-discipline is a journey of personal growth and empowerment. By developing the habits, mindset, and behaviors that support our goals and aspirations, we become the masters of our own destiny, capable of achieving greatness in any endeavor we pursue.

So, dear reader, I encourage you to embrace the practice of cultivating self-discipline in your own life. Set clear goals, develop healthy habits, manage your time effectively, and persevere in the face of challenges. For when you cultivate self-discipline, you unlock the key to mastery and open the dooSelf-discipline is the cornerstone of mastery, the guiding force that empowers individuals to stay focused, motivated, and committed to their goals despite challenges and distractions. In this chapter, we delve into the transformative journey of cultivating self-discipline and its profound impact on achieving mastery in all aspects of life.

At its essence, self-discipline is the ability to control one's thoughts, emotions, and actions in pursuit of a higher purpose or goal. It requires a steadfast commitment to one's values, principles, and aspirations, even in the face of temptation, adversity, or uncertainty.

One of the key components of cultivating self-discipline is setting clear goals and priorities. By identifying what is most important to us and aligning our actions with our values and aspirations, we create a roadmap for success that guides our decisions and actions with purpose and clarity.

Moreover, cultivating self-discipline involves developing healthy habits and routines that support our goals and aspirations. By establishing consistent practices such as time management, goal setting, and daily rituals, we create structure and discipline in our lives that enable us to stay focused and productive, even in the midst of distractions or challenges.

Another aspect of cultivating self-discipline is the ability to delay gratification and resist instant gratification in favor of long-term rewards. By practicing self-control and resisting impulses that detract from our goals, we strengthen our willpower and resilience, building the mental fortitude needed to overcome obstacles and persevere in the pursuit of mastery.

Furthermore, cultivating self-discipline requires self-awareness and accountability. By taking ownership of our actions and choices, we hold ourselves accountable for our progress and shortcomings, fostering a sense of responsibility and integrity that fuels our commitment to excellence.

In essence, cultivating self-discipline is a journey of self-mastery and personal growth. By setting clear goals, developing healthy habits, practicing self-control, and fostering self-awareness and accountability, we empower ourselves to overcome obstacles, achieve our aspirations, and reach our fullest potential.

So, dear reader, I encourage you to embrace the practice of cultivating self-discipline in your own life. Set clear goals, establish healthy habits, and practice self-control and accountability with unwavering commitment and determination. For when you cultivate self-discipline, you unlock the key to mastery and open the door to unlimited possibilities for success and fulfillment.

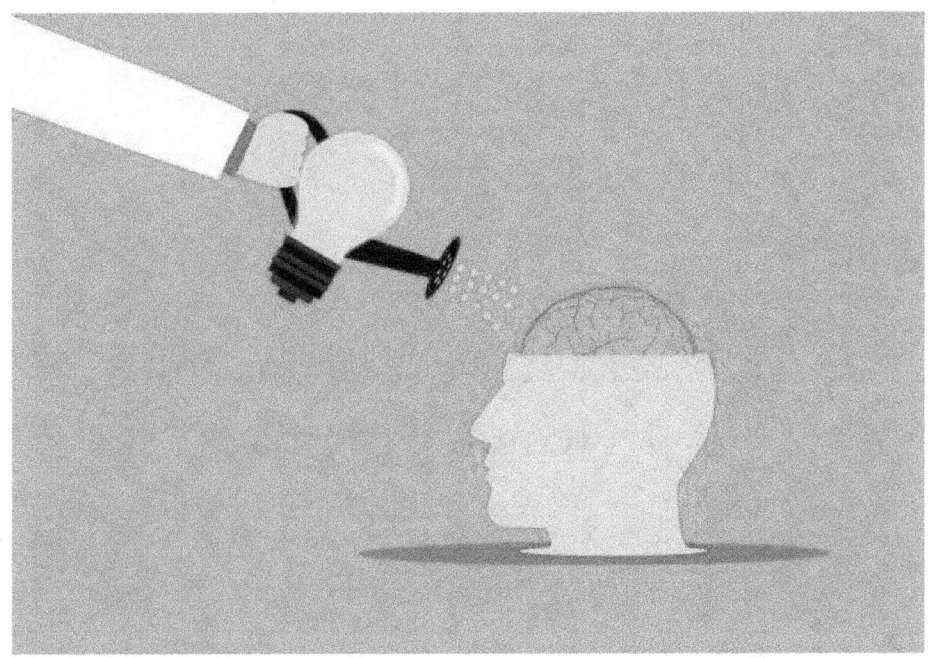

24

24

Transcending Procrastination: Overcoming Inertia

Procrastination, the silent enemy of progress, lurks in the shadows of our minds, whispering excuses and distractions that derail our best intentions. In this chapter, we explore the transformative journey of transcending procrastination and reclaiming our power to take action.

At its core, procrastination is a manifestation of fear, doubt, or discomfort that paralyzes us from taking action towards our goals. It is the tendency to delay or avoid tasks that are important or challenging, opting instead for temporary relief or distraction.

One of the key strategies for transcending procrastination is understanding its underlying causes. Procrastination often stems from fear of failure, perfectionism, overwhelm, or lack of clarity about our goals. By identifying the root cause of our procrastination, we can address it directly and develop strategies to overcome it.

Moreover, transcending procrastination involves breaking tasks down into smaller, more manageable steps. When faced with a daunting task, it's easy to feel overwhelmed and paralyzed by the enormity of the challenge. By breaking the task down into smaller, actionable steps, we make it easier to get started and build momentum towards completion.

Another effective strategy for transcending procrastination is creating a supportive environment that minimizes distractions and maximizes focus. This may involve setting up a dedicated workspace, eliminating sources of temptation or interruption, and establishing routines or rituals that signal to our brain that it's time to focus and work.

Furthermore, transcending procrastination requires cultivating self-awareness and practicing self-compassion. It's important to recognize that procrastination is a common human experience and that we're not alone in struggling with it. By treating ourselves with kindness and understanding, we can break free from the cycle of self-blame and self-criticism that often accompanies procrastination.

In essence, transcending procrastination is a journey of self-discovery and personal growth. By understanding its root causes, breaking tasks down into manageable steps, creating a supportive environment, and practicing self-awareness and self-compassion, we can reclaim our power to take action and move forward towards our goals.

So, dear reader, I encourage you to embrace the challenge of transcending procrastination in your own life. Take small steps, create a supportive environment, and be gentle with yourself as you navigate the ups and downs of the journey. For when we transcend procrastination, we unlock our full potential and open the door to limitless possibilities for growth and achievement.

Procrastination is the silent thief of time, robbing us of our productivity, potential, and peace of mind. In this chapter, we explore the transformative journey of transcending procrastination and reclaiming control over our time and actions.

At its core, procrastination is the tendency to delay or postpone tasks and responsibilities, often out of fear, uncertainty, or lack of motivation. It is a habit that can undermine our goals and aspirations, leaving us feeling overwhelmed, stressed, and unfulfilled.

One of the key strategies for transcending procrastination is understanding its root causes. Procrastination often stems from fear of failure, perfectionism, or overwhelm. By identifying the underlying reasons for our procrastination, we can address them directly and develop strategies to overcome them.

Moreover, transcending procrastination involves breaking tasks down into smaller, more manageable steps. Often, procrastination occurs when tasks feel overwhelming or daunting. By breaking tasks down into smaller, more manageable steps, we can reduce feelings of overwhelm and make progress towards our goals more manageable.

Another effective strategy for transcending procrastination is setting deadlines and holding ourselves accountable for meeting them. Deadlines create a sense of urgency and focus, motivating us to take action and prioritize our tasks more effectively.

Furthermore, transcending procrastination requires cultivating a mindset of self-compassion and resilience. It's important to recognize that procrastination is a common challenge that many people face and that it's okay to stumble along the way. By practicing self-compassion and treating ourselves with kindness and understanding, we can overcome setbacks and continue moving forward towards our goals.

In essence, transcending procrastination is a journey of self-awareness, self-compassion, and intentional action. By understanding the root causes of procrastination, breaking tasks down into manageable steps, setting deadlines, and practicing self-compassion, we can reclaim control over our time and actions and achieve our goals with greater ease and satisfaction.

So, dear reader, I encourage you to embark on the journey of transcending procrastination in your own life. Identify the underlying reasons for your procrastination, break tasks down into smaller steps, set deadlines, and practice self-compassion as you work towards overcoming inertia and reclaiming control over your time and actions. For when you transcend procrastination, you unlock the door to greater productivity, fulfillment, and success.

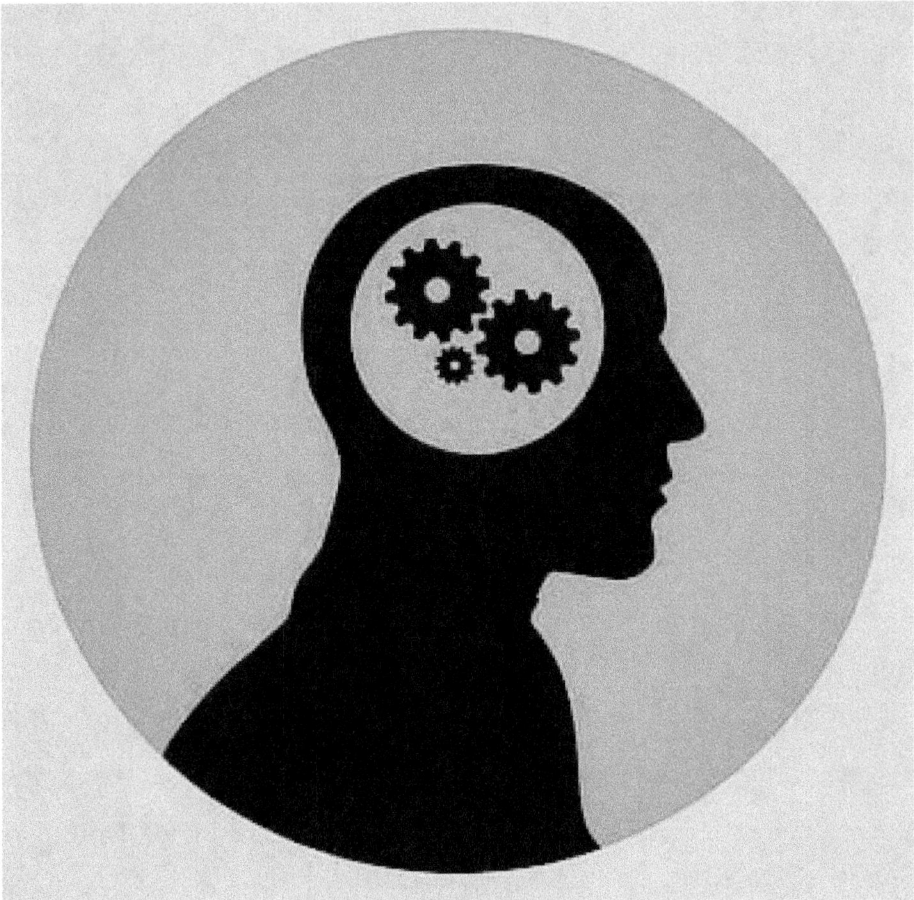

TRANSCENDING PROCRASTINATION: OVERCOMING INERTIA

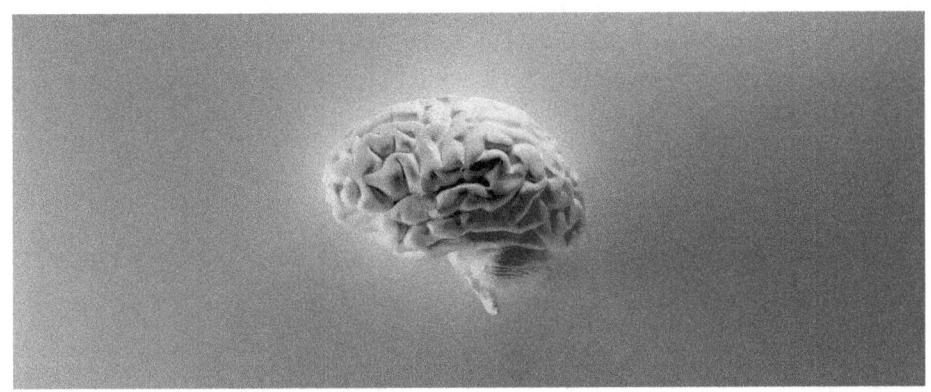

25

25

Building a Magnetic Personality: Attracting Success

A magnetic personality has the power to captivate and inspire others, drawing them towards success and creating opportunities for growth and fulfillment. In this chapter, we explore the art of building a magnetic personality and harnessing its transformative potential to attract success in all areas of life.

At the core of a magnetic personality lies authenticity - the genuine expression of one's true self, values, and passions. Authenticity resonates with others on a deep level, fostering trust, connection, and admiration. By embracing authenticity, we invite others to do the same, creating an environment of openness and authenticity that attracts success and abundance.

One of the key attributes of a magnetic personality is charisma - the ability to charm and influence others with warmth, confidence, and charisma. Charismatic individuals exude positivity, enthusiasm, and energy, drawing others towards them like moths to a flame. By cultivating charisma through self-confidence, self-awareness, and interpersonal skills, we can amplify our magnetic presence and attract success effortlessly.

Moreover, building a magnetic personality involves developing strong communication skills that allow us to connect with others on a deeper level.

Effective communicators listen actively, speak with clarity and conviction, and convey empathy and understanding in their interactions. By honing our communication skills, we can build rapport, inspire trust, and cultivate meaningful relationships that fuel our success.

Another aspect of building a magnetic personality is cultivating a positive mindset and attitude towards life. Positivity is infectious and has the power to uplift and inspire others, creating a ripple effect of positivity that attracts success and abundance. By cultivating a positive mindset through gratitude, optimism, and resilience, we can create a magnetic aura that draws opportunities and blessings into our lives.

Furthermore, building a magnetic personality involves nurturing emotional intelligence - the ability to understand and manage our emotions effectively and empathize with others. Emotional intelligence enables us to navigate social interactions with grace and tact, fostering deeper connections and mutual respect. By developing emotional intelligence, we can build trust, inspire loyalty, and attract success in all areas of life.

In essence, building a magnetic personality is a journey of self-discovery, self-expression, and personal growth. By embracing authenticity, cultivating charisma, honing communication skills, nurturing positivity, and developing emotional intelligence, we can unlock the full potential of our magnetic presence and attract success in abundance.

So, dear reader, I encourage you to embark on the journey of building a magnetic personality in your own life. Embrace authenticity, cultivate charisma, communicate with clarity and empathy, nurture positivity, and develop emotional intelligence. For when you radiate with the magnetic energy of your true self, you become a beacon of success and inspiration, drawing opportunities and blessings into your life effortlessly.

A magnetic personality exudes charisma, confidence, and authenticity, drawing others towards you and opening doors to opportunities. In this chapter, we explore the transformative journey of building a magnetic personality and how it can attract success in all areas of life.

At the heart of a magnetic personality lies self-awareness and self-confidence. Understanding your strengths, values, and passions allows you to project authenticity and integrity, which are magnetic qualities that attract others to you. Building self-confidence involves recognizing your worth and embracing your uniqueness, allowing you to shine brightly and inspire those around you.

One of the key components of building a magnetic personality is effective communication. Clear and confident communication fosters connection and rapport with others, making them more receptive to your ideas and goals. By honing your communication skills, you can convey your thoughts and emotions with clarity and conviction, leaving a lasting impression on those you encounter.

Moreover, building a magnetic personality involves cultivating a positive attitude and outlook on life. Optimism and enthusiasm are contagious qualities that draw people towards you and inspire them to align themselves with your vision and goals. By maintaining a positive mindset, you attract positive energy and opportunities into your life, creating a ripple effect of success and abundance.

Another aspect of building a magnetic personality is empathy and emotional intelligence. Being able to understand and connect with the emotions of others allows you to build deeper and more meaningful relationships. By listening actively and demonstrating empathy, you create a sense of trust and rapport that makes others feel valued and appreciated in your presence.

Furthermore, building a magnetic personality involves continuously learning and growing as an individual. Embracing new experiences, expanding your horizons, and seeking personal development opportunities allow you to evolve and become the best version of yourself. By investing in your growth and development, you enhance your magnetism and attract success on a deeper level.

In essence, building a magnetic personality is about embracing who you are, communicating with clarity and confidence, maintaining a positive attitude, and connecting authentically with others. By cultivating these qualities, you create a magnetic presence that draws success towards you effortlessly.

So, dear reader, I encourage you to embark on the journey of building a magnetic personality in your own life. Embrace your uniqueness, hone your communication skills, maintain a positive mindset, and cultivate empathy and emotional intelligence. For when you build a magnetic personality, you become a beacon of success and inspiration, attracting abundance and opportunities into your life with ease and grace.

26

26

The Power of Faith: Trusting in Your Vision

Faith is the unwavering belief in something greater than ourselves, the conviction that our dreams and aspirations are within reach, even in the face of uncertainty and doubt. In this chapter, we explore the transformative power of faith and its ability to propel us towards our vision of success.

At its core, faith is the foundation upon which dreams are built. It is the belief that our goals and aspirations are not merely wishful thinking but achievable realities waiting to be realized. Faith gives us the courage to pursue our dreams with conviction and resilience, knowing that setbacks and challenges are temporary detours on the path to success.

One of the key aspects of faith is trusting in our vision, even when it seems out of reach or impossible. Faith allows us to see beyond the limitations of our current circumstances and envision a future filled with possibility and potential. By trusting in our vision and taking inspired action towards our goals, we align ourselves with the energy of the universe and invite miracles to unfold in our lives.

Moreover, faith empowers us to overcome fear and doubt and embrace uncertainty with courage and grace. It is the antidote to self-doubt and negative self-talk, reminding us of our inherent worth and potential for greatness. By cultivating faith in ourselves and our abilities, we banish limiting beliefs and step into our power as creators of our own destiny.

Another aspect of faith is surrendering to the flow of life and trusting in divine timing. Faith teaches us that everything happens for a reason and that the universe has a plan for us, even if we can't see it in the moment. By surrendering to the wisdom of the universe and trusting in its guidance, we release the need for control and open ourselves up to the infinite possibilities that lie ahead.

Furthermore, faith fosters a sense of gratitude and abundance, reminding us of the blessings and opportunities that surround us. By cultivating an attitude of gratitude, we attract more blessings into our lives and amplify the power of our faith to manifest our desires.

In essence, the power of faith is the fuel that propels us towards our vision of success. By trusting in our vision, overcoming fear and doubt, surrendering to divine timing, and cultivating gratitude, we align ourselves with the energy of the universe and invite miracles to unfold in our lives.

So, dear reader, I encourage you to embrace the power of faith in your own life. Trust in your vision, overcome fear and doubt, surrender to divine timing, and cultivate an attitude of gratitude. For when you have faith, anything is possible, and theFaith is the unwavering belief in the fulfillment of your vision, even in the face of uncertainty and doubt. In this chapter, we explore the transformative power of faith and its profound impact on turning dreams into reality.

At its core, faith is the cornerstone of manifestation, the fuel that propels your aspirations forward and infuses them with energy and purpose. It is the unwavering trust in the inherent goodness of the universe and the belief that your dreams are within reach, no matter the obstacles that may arise.

One of the key aspects of harnessing the power of faith is clarity of vision. By clearly defining your goals and aspirations, you create a roadmap for success that guides your actions and decisions with purpose and intention. With a clear vision in mind, you can cultivate faith in your ability to achieve your dreams, even when the path ahead seems uncertain or challenging.

Moreover, faith involves surrendering to the flow of life and trusting in

THE POWER OF FAITH: TRUSTING IN YOUR VISION

divine timing. It is the willingness to release control and allow the universe to work its magic, knowing that everything is unfolding exactly as it should. By relinquishing the need for certainty and embracing the unknown, you open yourself up to infinite possibilities and opportunities for growth and expansion.

Another aspect of the power of faith is resilience in the face of adversity. Faith allows you to persevere in the pursuit of your goals, even when faced with setbacks or obstacles along the way. By maintaining unwavering belief in your vision and trusting in your ability to overcome challenges, you cultivate the resilience needed to weather any storm and emerge stronger and more resilient than ever before.

Furthermore, faith is a source of inspiration and motivation that fuels your journey towards success. It is the inner fire that propels you forward with passion and determination, reminding you of the limitless potential that lies within you. With faith as your guide, you can navigate the ups and downs of life with grace and ease, knowing that every challenge is an opportunity for growth and expansion.

In essence, the power of faith is the key to unlocking the door to your wildest dreams and aspirations. By cultivating unwavering belief in yourself and your vision, you can manifest miracles in your life and create the reality you desire.

So, dear reader, I encourage you to embrace the power of faith in your own life. Trust in your vision, surrender to the flow of life, and cultivate resilience in the face of adversity. For when you have faith, anything is possible, and the universe conspires to support you in manifesting your dreams into reality.

universe conspires to help you achieve your dreams.

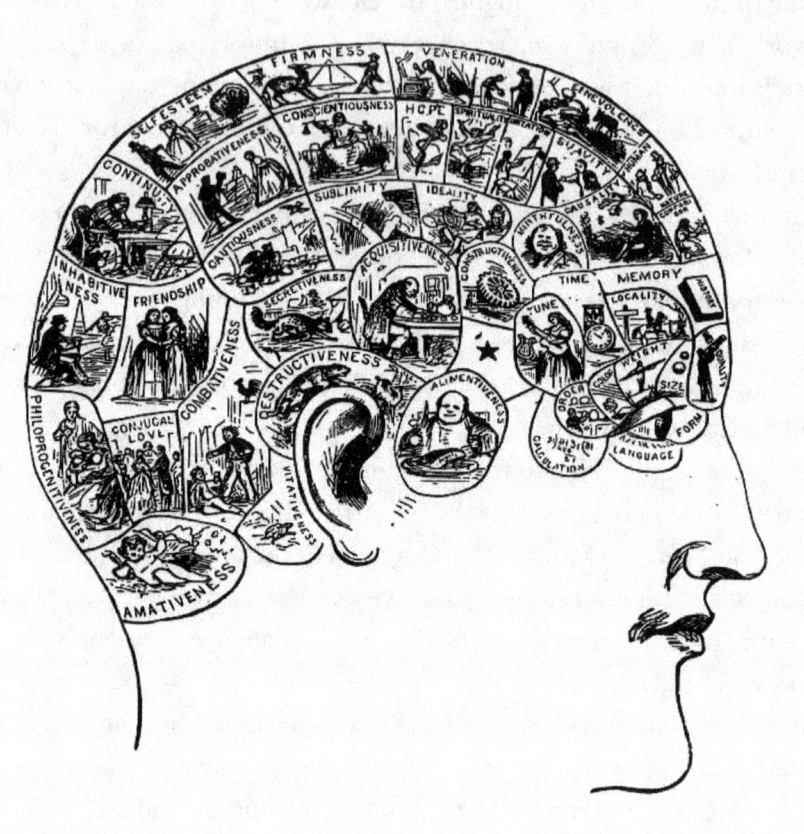

27

27

Creating Your Master Plan: Designing Your Destiny

Your master plan is the blueprint for the life you envision, guiding your actions and choices as you journey towards your dreams. In this chapter, we explore the transformative process of creating your master plan and taking deliberate steps to design your destiny.

At its core, creating your master plan involves clarity of vision and purpose. Take the time to reflect on your values, passions, and aspirations, and envision the life you desire to create. Define your goals with precision, outlining both short-term milestones and long-term objectives that align with your deepest desires.

Moreover, creating your master plan requires strategic thinking and planning. Break down your goals into actionable steps, identifying the resources, skills, and support systems you need to achieve them. Consider potential obstacles and challenges, and develop contingency plans to navigate them with grace and resilience.

Another aspect of creating your master plan is accountability and commitment. Hold yourself accountable to your goals by setting deadlines and milestones, and track your progress regularly to stay on course. Surround yourself with supportive allies who can hold you accountable and provide encouragement and guidance along the way.

Furthermore, creating your master plan involves flexibility and adaptability. Life is unpredictable, and circumstances may change along the way. Remain open to new opportunities and possibilities, and be willing to adjust your plans as needed to stay aligned with your vision and values.

In essence, creating your master plan is a dynamic and ongoing process that empowers you to take ownership of your life and design your destiny with intention and purpose. By clarifying your vision, planning strategically, holding yourself accountable, and remaining flexible and adaptable, you can manifest the life of your dreams and create a legacy that inspires generations to come.

So, dear reader, I encourage you to embark on the journey of creating your master plan. Take the time to reflect on your values and aspirations, and define your goals with clarity and precision. Develop a strategic plan of action, hold yourself accountable, and remain flexible and adaptable as you navigate the twists and turns of your journey. For when you create your master plan, you take control of your destiny and unlock the infinite possibilities that await you.

Your master plan is the blueprint for your destiny, the roadmap that guides you towards your greatest aspirations and dreams. In this chapter, we explore the transformative process of creating your master plan and taking deliberate steps towards the life you desire.

At its core, creating your master plan involves clarity of vision and purpose. It requires deep reflection on your values, passions, and long-term goals, allowing you to define the life you want to live and the person you want to become. With a clear vision in mind, you can create a roadmap that aligns your actions and decisions with your highest aspirations.

One of the key aspects of creating your master plan is setting specific, measurable, achievable, relevant, and time-bound (SMART) goals. By breaking your vision down into smaller, actionable steps, you can create momentum and track your progress towards your desired outcomes. SMART goals provide clarity and focus, empowering you to take consistent action towards your dreams.

Moreover, creating your master plan involves identifying potential obsta-

CREATING YOUR MASTER PLAN: DESIGNING YOUR DESTINY

cles and challenges that may arise along the way. By anticipating potential roadblocks, you can develop strategies to overcome them and stay resilient in the face of adversity. With a proactive mindset and a willingness to adapt, you can navigate challenges with grace and confidence, knowing that every obstacle is an opportunity for growth.

Another aspect of creating your master plan is cultivating a mindset of abundance and possibility. Instead of focusing on limitations or perceived barriers, focus on the limitless potential that lies within you. By embracing a mindset of abundance, you open yourself up to infinite opportunities and possibilities, allowing you to manifest your dreams into reality with ease and grace.

Furthermore, creating your master plan involves taking consistent and deliberate action towards your goals. It's not enough to simply set goals and create a plan; you must take action each day to move closer to your desired outcomes. By prioritizing your goals, managing your time effectively, and staying focused on your vision, you can make steady progress towards your dreams and aspirations.

In essence, creating your master plan is about taking ownership of your life and intentionally designing the future you desire. By defining your vision, setting SMART goals, anticipating challenges, cultivating abundance, and taking consistent action, you can create the life of your dreams and fulfill your highest potential.

So, dear reader, I encourage you to embark on the journey of creating your master plan. Take the time to reflect on your vision and values, set SMART goals, anticipate challenges, cultivate abundance, and take consistent action towards your dreams. For when you create your master plan, you take control of your destiny and design a life that is truly aligned with your deepest desires and aspirations.

THE POWER

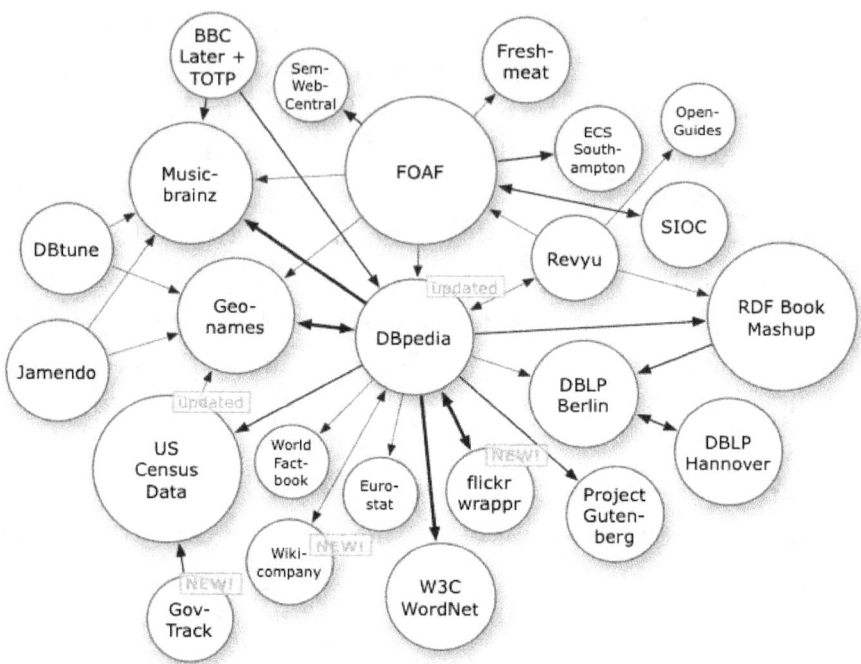

28

The Power of Giving: Cultivating Abundance Mentality

Giving is not only an act of generosity but also a powerful mindset that cultivates abundance and prosperity in our lives. In this chapter, we explore the transformative impact of giving and how it nurtures an abundance mentality that attracts greater success and fulfillment.

At its core, giving is an expression of abundance mentality—a belief that there is more than enough to go around and that by sharing our resources, talents, and kindness, we enrich not only the lives of others but also our own. Cultivating an abundance mentality shifts our focus from scarcity and lack to abundance and plenty, allowing us to approach life with optimism, gratitude, and generosity.

One of the key aspects of the power of giving is the ripple effect it creates. When we give freely and generously, we create a positive energy that radiates outward, touching the lives of everyone we encounter. Acts of kindness and generosity have a way of inspiring others to pay it forward, creating a ripple effect of goodness and abundance that spreads far and wide.

Moreover, giving fosters a sense of connection and community. When we give to others, we strengthen our bonds with them and create a sense of belonging and unity. By nurturing relationships built on trust, respect, and reciprocity, we create a supportive network of allies and collaborators who uplift and empower one another on the journey towards success and fulfillment.

Another aspect of the power of giving is its ability to shift our perspective and mindset. By focusing on the needs and well-being of others, we shift our attention away from our own worries and concerns, gaining a broader perspective on life and a deeper appreciation for the blessings we have. Giving allows us to tap into a reservoir of gratitude and abundance that transforms how we perceive ourselves and the world around us.

Furthermore, giving is a source of joy and fulfillment that transcends material wealth or possessions. The act of giving, whether it's through donating our time, resources, or talents, fills our hearts with a sense of purpose and meaning that money can't buy. By giving freely and generously, we experience a deep sense of fulfillment and satisfaction that enriches our lives in profound ways.

In essence, the power of giving lies in its ability to nurture an abundance mentality that attracts greater success, fulfillment, and prosperity into our lives. By embracing a mindset of generosity, gratitude, and abundance, we create a ripple effect of goodness that uplifts and empowers everyone around us.

So, dear reader, I encourage you to embrace the power of giving in your own life. Whether it's through acts of kindness, generosity, or service to others, find ways to give freely and abundantly. For when you cultivate an abundance mentality through giving, you open yourself up to a world of limitless possibilities and opportunities for success and fulfillment.

Giving is not just an act of kindness; it's a powerful force that cultivates an abundance mentality and enriches both the giver and the receiver. In this chapter, we explore the transformative impact of giving and how it can unlock the flow of abundance in our lives.

At its core, giving is an expression of generosity, compassion, and gratitude. It is the act of sharing our time, resources, and talents with others without expecting anything in return. When we give freely and selflessly, we tap into the infinite abundance of the universe and open ourselves up to receiving blessings in return.

THE POWER OF GIVING: CULTIVATING ABUNDANCE MENTALITY

One of the key aspects of giving is its ability to shift our mindset from scarcity to abundance. In a world where scarcity mindset often prevails, giving reminds us that there is always enough to go around and that abundance is a mindset that can be cultivated. By giving freely and trusting in the abundance of the universe, we attract more blessings into our lives and create a positive ripple effect that impacts both ourselves and others.

Moreover, giving fosters a sense of connection and belonging within our communities. When we give to others, we create bonds of trust and reciprocity that strengthen the fabric of society. By supporting one another and lifting each other up, we create a culture of abundance where everyone has the opportunity to thrive and succeed.

Another aspect of the power of giving is its ability to bring joy and fulfillment into our lives. Research has shown that acts of kindness and generosity can have a profound impact on our mental and emotional well-being, boosting our mood, reducing stress, and increasing our overall sense of happiness and satisfaction. When we give from the heart, we experience a deep sense of fulfillment that transcends material wealth and leaves a lasting legacy of love and compassion.

Furthermore, giving is a powerful tool for manifesting our desires and goals. When we give freely and generously, we send a powerful message to the universe that we trust in its abundance and are open to receiving blessings in return. By giving with an open heart and a spirit of gratitude, we create a positive energetic flow that attracts more abundance into our lives and accelerates the manifestation of our dreams.

In essence, the power of giving lies in its ability to transform lives, foster abundance, and create a more compassionate and connected world. By cultivating a mindset of generosity, compassion, and gratitude, we tap into the infinite abundance of the universe and unlock the flow of blessings into our lives.

So, dear reader, I encourage you to embrace the power of giving in your own life. Look for opportunities to give freely and generously to others, whether through acts of kindness, donations, or volunteering. By giving from the heart and trusting in the abundance of the universe, you can create a life filled with joy, fulfillment, and abundance beyond measure.

29

29

Overcoming Adversity: Turning Challenges into Opportunities

Adversity is an inevitable part of life, but it's also a powerful catalyst for growth and transformation. In this chapter, we'll explore the transformative journey of overcoming adversity and turning challenges into opportunities for personal and professional development.

At its core, overcoming adversity requires resilience, perseverance, and a positive mindset. It's about facing challenges head-on, learning from setbacks, and using them as stepping stones towards success. When we embrace adversity as an opportunity for growth rather than a roadblock, we unlock our full potential and emerge stronger, wiser, and more resilient than ever before.

One of the key strategies for overcoming adversity is reframing our mindset and perspective. Instead of viewing challenges as insurmountable obstacles, see them as opportunities for growth and learning. By shifting our mindset from one of fear and resistance to one of curiosity and possibility, we open ourselves up to new insights, solutions, and opportunities that can help us overcome adversity with grace and resilience.

Moreover, overcoming adversity involves developing coping strategies and resilience-building techniques to navigate challenging times effectively. This may include practicing self-care, seeking support from others, setting boundaries, and cultivating a strong support network of friends, family, and mentors who can provide guidance and encouragement during difficult times.

Another aspect of overcoming adversity is embracing failure as a natural part of the learning process. Failure is not the end of the road but rather a stepping stone towards success. By reframing failure as feedback and using it as an opportunity to learn, grow, and improve, we can turn setbacks into opportunities for growth and development.

Furthermore, overcoming adversity requires taking proactive steps towards problem-solving and goal-setting. Instead of dwelling on the challenges we face, focus on finding solutions and taking decisive action towards achieving our goals. By breaking tasks down into manageable steps and taking consistent action, we can overcome even the most daunting obstacles and emerge victorious in the face of adversity.

In essence, overcoming adversity is a journey of self-discovery, resilience, and growth. By reframing our mindset, developing resilience-building techniques, embracing failure as feedback, and taking proactive steps towards problem-solving and goal-setting, we can turn challenges into opportunities for personal and professional development.

So, dear reader, I encourage you to embrace the power of overcoming adversity in your own life. See challenges as opportunities for growth, develop resilience-building techniques, and take proactive steps towards achieving your goals. For when we embrace adversity as a catalyst for growth, we unlock our full potential and create a life filled with purpose, resilience, and abundance.

Adversity is an inevitable part of life, but it is also a powerful catalyst for growth and transformation. In this chapter, we explore the transformative journey of overcoming adversity and turning challenges into opportunities for personal and professional development.

At its core, overcoming adversity requires resilience, courage, and a willingness to confront obstacles head-on. It is about facing adversity with grace and determination, refusing to be defined or defeated by the challenges we encounter.

One of the key aspects of overcoming adversity is maintaining a positive mindset. Instead of viewing challenges as insurmountable obstacles, see them as opportunities for growth and learning. By adopting a growth mindset and reframing adversity as a chance to strengthen your resilience and resourcefulness, you can approach challenges with confidence and optimism.

Moreover, overcoming adversity involves seeking support from others and building a strong network of allies and mentors. Surround yourself with people who uplift and inspire you, and lean on them for guidance and encouragement when facing difficult times. By connecting with others who have overcome similar challenges, you can gain valuable insights and perspectives that help you navigate adversity with greater ease and resilience.

Another aspect of overcoming adversity is perseverance and determination. Despite setbacks and obstacles, remain committed to your goals and continue moving forward with unwavering determination. Remember that setbacks are not failures but opportunities to learn and grow stronger. By persevering in the face of adversity, you build the resilience and tenacity needed to overcome any challenge that comes your way.

Furthermore, overcoming adversity involves embracing change and embracing the opportunity to adapt and evolve. Life is full of unexpected twists and turns, and it's essential to remain flexible and open-minded in the face of adversity. Instead of resisting change, embrace it as an opportunity to explore new possibilities and discover hidden strengths and talents within yourself.

In essence, overcoming adversity is a journey of self-discovery, resilience, and growth. By maintaining a positive mindset, seeking support from others, persevering in the face of challenges, and embracing change, you can turn adversity into an opportunity for personal and professional development.

So, dear reader, I encourage you to embrace the challenges you encounter in life as opportunities for growth and transformation. Face adversity with courage and determination, knowing that every obstacle you overcome brings you one step closer to realizing your fullest potential. For when you overcome adversity, you emerge stronger, wiser, and more resilient than ever before, ready to seize the opportunities that lie ahead.

THE POWER

Fixed

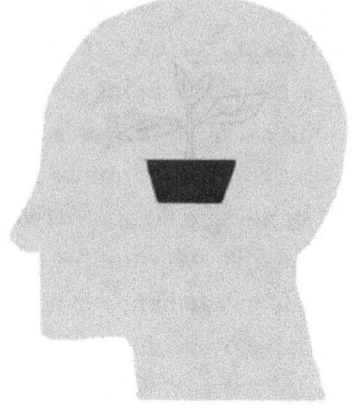

Growth

30

30

The Power of Gratitude: Fostering Prosperity Consciousness

Gratitude is a potent force that cultivates prosperity consciousness and transforms our perception of abundance. In this chapter, we delve into the profound impact of gratitude and how it shapes our experiences of wealth and abundance.

At its essence, gratitude is the practice of acknowledging and appreciating the blessings, big and small, that enrich our lives. It is a mindset that shifts our focus from what we lack to what we have, fostering a sense of contentment, fulfillment, and abundance.

One of the key aspects of gratitude is its ability to amplify the positive aspects of our lives. By consciously focusing on the things we are grateful for, we invite more blessings into our lives and create a positive feedback loop of abundance. When we approach life with an attitude of gratitude, we attract more reasons to be grateful, creating a virtuous cycle of prosperity and fulfillment.

Moreover, gratitude is a powerful tool for shifting our perspective during challenging times. When we face adversity or setbacks, it can be easy to dwell on what's going wrong and overlook the blessings that still surround us. However, by practicing gratitude, we can reframe our challenges as opportunities for growth and learning, recognizing the silver linings amidst the storm clouds.

Another aspect of the power of gratitude is its ability to enhance our relationships and connections with others. When we express gratitude towards others, we strengthen our bonds and foster a sense of trust, respect, and appreciation. By acknowledging the contributions and kindness of those around us, we create a supportive network of allies and collaborators who uplift and inspire us on our journey towards success.

Furthermore, gratitude is a potent antidote to the scarcity mindset that often permeates our culture. Instead of dwelling on what we lack or comparing ourselves to others, gratitude reminds us of the abundance that already exists in our lives. By shifting our focus from scarcity to abundance, we open ourselves up to infinite possibilities and opportunities for growth and expansion.

In essence, the power of gratitude lies in its ability to transform our lives from the inside out. By cultivating an attitude of gratitude, we shift our perception of abundance and invite more blessings into our lives. Gratitude is not just a feeling; it is a way of being that enriches every aspect of our lives and opens the door to unlimited prosperity and fulfillment.

So, dear reader, I encourage you to embrace the power of gratitude in your own life. Take time each day to reflect on the blessings that surround you and express gratitude for them. Whether through journaling, meditation, or acts of kindness towards others, cultivate an attitude of gratitude that fosters prosperity consciousness and attracts abundance into your life. For when you live with gratitude, you live with an open heart and an abundance of blessings that enrich every moment of your life.

Gratitude is not just a simple expression of thanks; it's a transformative force that cultivates prosperity consciousness and attracts abundance into our lives. In this chapter, we explore the profound impact of gratitude and how it can shift our mindset towards abundance and prosperity.

At its core, gratitude is the practice of acknowledging and appreciating the blessings and abundance that surround us, both big and small. It is the recognition that every moment, every experience, and every person in our lives is a gift to be cherished and celebrated. By cultivating an attitude of

THE POWER OF GRATITUDE: FOSTERING PROSPERITY CONSCIOUSNESS

gratitude, we open ourselves up to the abundance that already exists within and around us.

One of the key aspects of the power of gratitude is its ability to shift our mindset from scarcity to abundance. Instead of focusing on what we lack or what is missing from our lives, gratitude allows us to recognize and celebrate the abundance that is already present. By acknowledging the blessings in our lives, we attract more blessings into our experience, creating a positive feedback loop of abundance and prosperity.

Moreover, gratitude fosters a sense of contentment and fulfillment in our lives. When we focus on the things we are grateful for, we shift our attention away from what we don't have and towards what we do have. This shift in perspective allows us to find joy and satisfaction in the present moment, regardless of our external circumstances.

Another aspect of the power of gratitude is its ability to improve our mental and emotional well-being. Research has shown that practicing gratitude can reduce stress, increase happiness, and improve overall quality of life. By focusing on the positive aspects of our lives and expressing gratitude for them, we cultivate a sense of inner peace and happiness that radiates outwards, positively impacting our relationships and interactions with others.

Furthermore, gratitude is a powerful tool for manifesting our desires and goals. When we approach life with an attitude of gratitude, we send a powerful message to the universe that we appreciate and value the blessings in our lives. This attitude of appreciation and abundance attracts more blessings into our experience, accelerating the manifestation of our dreams and aspirations.

In essence, the power of gratitude lies in its ability to shift our mindset towards abundance and prosperity. By cultivating an attitude of gratitude, we open ourselves up to the abundance that already exists within and around us, attracting more blessings into our lives and creating a ripple effect of positivity and prosperity.

So, dear reader, I encourage you to embrace the power of gratitude in your own life. Take a moment each day to acknowledge and appreciate the blessings in your life, both big and small. By cultivating an attitude of gratitude, you can foster prosperity consciousness and attract abundance into every area of your life.

GROW YOUR PEOPLE

31

31

Living Your Legacy: Embracing Fulfillment and Contribution

Living your legacy is about more than leaving behind material possessions or achievements; it's about creating a lasting impact and contributing to the greater good. In this chapter, we explore the transformative journey of embracing fulfillment and making meaningful contributions that leave a legacy of positivity and inspiration.

At its core, living your legacy is about aligning your actions and values with a sense of purpose and meaning. It involves reflecting on what matters most to you and how you want to be remembered, both personally and professionally. By living in alignment with your values and aspirations, you create a legacy that reflects your deepest desires and leaves a positive impact on the world.

One of the key aspects of living your legacy is embracing fulfillment and happiness in every aspect of your life. Instead of chasing external markers of success or validation, focus on cultivating inner peace, joy, and contentment. By living authentically and prioritizing your well-being, you create a legacy of happiness and fulfillment that inspires others to do the same.

Moreover, living your legacy involves making meaningful contributions to the world around you. Whether through acts of kindness, philanthropy, or advocacy, find ways to use your talents and resources to make a positive difference in the lives of others. By giving back to your community and leaving a legacy of service and compassion, you create a ripple effect of goodness that extends far beyond your lifetime.

Another aspect of living your legacy is fostering meaningful relationships and connections with others. Take the time to nurture your relationships with family, friends, and colleagues, and invest in building strong bonds of love and support. By leaving behind a legacy of love and connection, you create a lasting impact that transcends material wealth or achievements.

Furthermore, living your legacy involves embracing growth and learning throughout your life. Stay curious, open-minded, and willing to explore new ideas and experiences. By continuously evolving and expanding your horizons, you inspire others to embrace change and pursue their own paths of personal and professional development.

In essence, living your legacy is about embracing fulfillment, making meaningful contributions, fostering connections, and embracing growth and learning. By living authentically and in alignment with your values, you create a legacy that reflects your deepest desires and inspires others to live with purpose and meaning.

So, dear reader, I encourage you to embrace the journey of living your legacy in your own life. Reflect on what matters most to you, prioritize your well-being, and find ways to make meaningful contributions to the world around you. By living with intention and purpose, you can create a legacy that leaves a lasting impact and inspires future generations to do the same.

Living your legacy is about more than leaving behind a tangible inheritance; it's about the impact you make on the world and the lives you touch along the way. In this chapter, we explore the transformative journey of living your legacy and embracing fulfillment and contribution in every aspect of your life.

At its core, living your legacy is about aligning your actions and values with a greater purpose or mission that extends beyond your own lifetime. It's about living with intention and making choices that reflect your deepest values and aspirations. By living your legacy, you create a ripple effect of positive change that extends far beyond your immediate sphere of influence.

One of the key aspects of living your legacy is clarity of purpose. Take the time to reflect on what matters most to you and what kind of impact you want to make in the world. Define your values, passions, and goals, and let them guide your decisions and actions each day. By living in alignment with your purpose, you create a life of meaning and fulfillment that inspires others to do the same.

Moreover, living your legacy involves cultivating a mindset of abundance and generosity. Instead of focusing solely on personal gain or achievement, look for opportunities to contribute to the well-being of others and the greater good. Whether through acts of kindness, volunteer work, or philanthropy, find ways to give back and make a positive impact in the world. By living with an open heart and a spirit of generosity, you create a legacy of compassion and service that enriches the lives of those around you.

Another aspect of living your legacy is leading by example. Be the change you wish to see in the world, and inspire others to follow in your footsteps. Whether in your professional life, your personal relationships, or your community involvement, strive to embody the values and principles you hold dear. By living authentically and with integrity, you empower others to do the same and create a legacy of leadership and influence that extends far beyond your own lifetime.

Furthermore, living your legacy involves embracing the present moment and making the most of every opportunity to create a positive impact. Life is short and precious, and every moment is an opportunity to make a difference in the world. Seize each day with gratitude and purpose, and approach every interaction with kindness, compassion, and empathy. By living fully and authentically in the present moment, you create a legacy of love and connection that transcends time and space.

In essence, living your legacy is about embracing fulfillment and contribution in every aspect of your life. By aligning your actions with your values and purpose, cultivating a mindset of abundance and generosity, leading by example, and embracing the present moment, you can create a legacy of impact and inspiration that lasts for generations to come.

So, dear reader, I encourage you to embrace the journey of living your legacy in your own life. Reflect on your values and purpose, and make choices that align with your deepest aspirations. By living with intention and making a positive impact in the world, you can create a legacy of fulfillment and contribution that leaves a lasting imprint on the hearts and minds of others.

Growth Hacking Mindset

✓ Vždy otevřen novým možnostem
✓ Rozhodování na základě dat
✓ Vysoká digitální inteligence

LIVING YOUR LEGACY: EMBRACING FULFILLMENT AND CONTRIBUTION

32

32

"Desire: The Starting Point of All Achievement"

Desire is the spark that ignites the flame of achievement. It is the driving force behind every great accomplishment, the fuel that propels us forward in pursuit of our dreams. Without desire, there is no motivation, no direction, no purpose.

Desire is more than just a fleeting wish or passing fancy; it is a burning passion that consumes us, compelling us to take action and strive for greatness. It is the inner fire that pushes us beyond our limits, urging us to push through obstacles and setbacks on the path to success.

When desire takes hold of our hearts and minds, it transforms us. It gives us clarity of purpose, focusing our energy and attention on what truly matters. It empowers us to overcome fear and doubt, to persevere in the face of adversity, and to never settle for anything less than our dreams.

Desire is the first step on the journey to achievement, the catalyst that sets everything else in motion. It is the foundation upon which we build our goals and aspirations, the driving force behind every decision and action we take.

But desire alone is not enough; it must be coupled with determination, discipline, and dedication. It requires us to make sacrifices, to prioritize our goals above all else, and to never lose sight of what we truly want.

In the words of Napoleon Hill, "The starting point of all achievement is desire. Keep this constantly in mind. Weak desire brings weak results, just as a small fire makes a small amount of heat."

So let your desire burn brightly within you. Let it guide you, inspire you, and propel you toward the life of your dreams. For with desire as your compass, there is no limit to what you can achieve.

Desire is the ignition spark that propels us towards our goals and dreams. It's the fuel that drives us to take action, to strive for something greater than what we currently possess. Without desire, there would be no ambition, no motivation to improve ourselves or our circumstances.

Desire is not merely a fleeting wish or whim; it is a deep-seated longing that stirs within us, urging us to pursue our aspirations relentlessly. It is the seed from which all achievement springs forth.

When we cultivate a burning desire for something, we unleash a powerful force within ourselves. This force compels us to overcome obstacles, to push through setbacks, and to persist in the face of adversity. It fuels our determination and gives us the strength to persevere when the journey becomes challenging.

History is replete with examples of individuals who achieved greatness because they possessed an unwavering desire for success. From inventors and entrepreneurs to artists and athletes, those who have left an indelible mark on the world were driven by a burning passion to realize their dreams.

However, desire alone is not enough. It must be accompanied by belief in oneself and a willingness to take decisive action. We must have faith in our ability to achieve our goals and be willing to do whatever it takes to make them a reality.

In the words of Napoleon Hill, "Whatever the mind of man can conceive and believe, it can achieve." It is our desires that shape our destinies, and it is our willingness to pursue them with unwavering determination that ultimately leads us to success.

THE POWER

33

33

Faith: Visualizing and Believing in the Attainment of Desire

Faith is the bedrock upon which the edifice of achievement is built. It is the unwavering belief in the realization of our desires, even when the path ahead seems obscured by doubt or uncertainty. Like a beacon in the night, faith guides us through the darkest moments of our journey, illuminating the way forward with its radiant light.

At its core, faith is about seeing beyond the present circumstances and envisioning a future where our desires have become reality. It is the ability to visualize our goals with such clarity and conviction that they feel within our grasp, no matter how distant they may seem.

When we have faith in ourselves and our abilities, we tap into a reservoir of untapped potential. We cultivate a sense of inner certainty that propels us forward, even in the face of adversity. With faith as our companion, we are able to transcend the limitations of our circumstances and manifest our deepest desires into existence.

Visualization is a powerful tool for harnessing the power of faith. By creating vivid mental images of our desired outcomes, we imprint them onto our subconscious minds, making them seem more attainable and real. As we visualize our goals with increasing clarity and detail, we reinforce our belief in their attainment, making them all the more likely to come to fruition.

But faith is not just about wishful thinking or blind optimism. It is about taking inspired action towards our goals, trusting that our efforts will yield the desired results. It is about persevering in the face of obstacles and setbacks, knowing that every challenge is an opportunity for growth and learning.

In the words of Napoleon Hill, "Faith is the starting point of all accumulation of riches!" It is faith that gives birth to our desires and faith that sustains us on the journey to their fulfillment. With unwavering faith as our guide, there is no limit to what Faith is the unwavering belief in the fulfillment of our desires, even when circumstances may seem bleak or uncertain. It is the inner conviction that propels us forward, despite any doubts or obstacles that may stand in our way.

Visualizing our desires is a powerful tool that helps to crystallize our goals in our minds. By creating vivid mental images of what we wish to achieve, we are able to imbue our desires with a sense of reality and urgency. These mental pictures serve as beacons, guiding us towards our intended destination and inspiring us to take action.

But visualizing alone is not enough; we must also believe wholeheartedly in the attainment of our desires. Faith is the cornerstone upon which our dreams are built. It is the unwavering confidence that sustains us through difficult times and fuels our determination to press onward.

When we believe in the realization of our desires, we align ourselves with the infinite power of the universe. We tap into a reservoir of energy and creativity that enables us to overcome any obstacle and achieve the seemingly impossible.

Faith is not a passive state of mind; it is an active force that compels us to take bold and decisive action. It is the courage to step outside of our comfort zones and pursue our dreams with relentless passion and determination.

In the words of Napoleon Hill, "What the mind can conceive and believe, it can achieve." Faith is the catalyst that transforms our dreams into reality. By visualizing our desires and believing in their attainment, we unleash the full potential of our minds and unlock the limitless possibilities that lie within us.we can achieve.

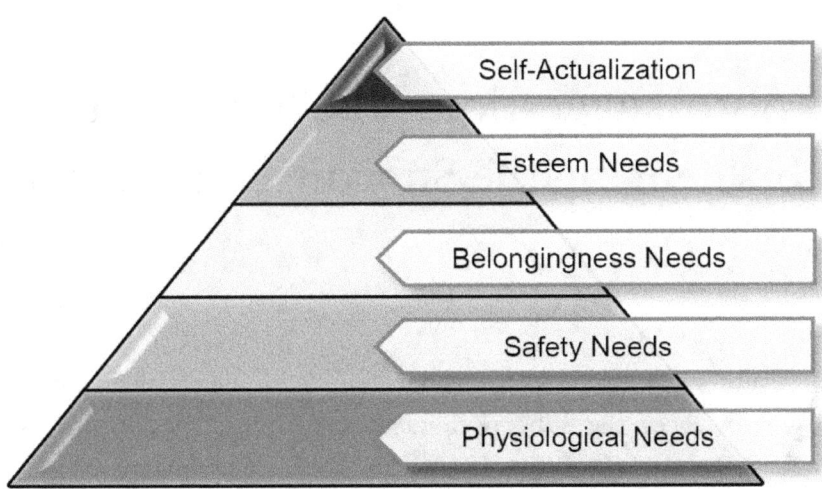

34

34

Auto-suggestion: The Medium for Influencing the Subconscious Mind

Auto-suggestion is a powerful technique for harnessing the immense power of the subconscious mind. It involves the deliberate repetition of positive affirmations or suggestions to oneself, with the intention of influencing our thoughts, beliefs, and behaviors on a subconscious level.

Our subconscious mind is like a fertile garden, ready to receive and nurture whatever seeds we plant within it. Through the practice of auto-suggestion, we can plant seeds of positivity, confidence, and success, which will then grow and flourish over time.

The key to effective auto-suggestion lies in the repetition and consistency of our affirmations. By repeatedly affirming our desired outcomes in a clear and concise manner, we can gradually reprogram our subconscious mind to align with our goals and aspirations.

Auto-suggestion works by bypassing the critical faculty of the conscious mind and directly accessing the subconscious. This allows us to instill new beliefs and attitudes that are in harmony with our desires, thus paving the way for their manifestation in our lives.

Moreover, auto-suggestion can be combined with visualization to enhance its effectiveness. By vividly imagining ourselves achieving our goals while affirming them to ourselves, we create a powerful synergy that amplifies the impact of our suggestions on the subconscious mind.

In essence, auto-suggestion is a tool that empowers us to take control of our thoughts and beliefs, thereby shaping our reality according to our desires. By harnessing the power of our subconscious mind through the practice of auto-suggestion, we can unlock our full potential and create the life we truly desire.

Auto-suggestion is a powerful tool for harnessing the latent potential of the subconscious mind. It is the practice of repeating positive affirmations or suggestions to oneself in order to instill certain beliefs or behaviors.

Our subconscious mind is like a vast reservoir of untapped resources, containing the blueprint for our beliefs, attitudes, and habits. By employing auto-suggestion, we can imprint new patterns of thought and behavior onto this subconscious canvas, thereby reshaping our reality from the inside out.

The key to effective auto-suggestion lies in repetition and consistency. By consistently feeding our minds with positive affirmations and suggestions, we gradually reprogram our subconscious to align with our conscious desires and goals.

Through auto-suggestion, we can cultivate a mindset of abundance, confidence, and success. We can overwrite limiting beliefs and replace them with empowering ones. We can train our minds to focus on solutions rather than problems, and to see opportunities where others see obstacles.

But auto-suggestion is not merely a matter of reciting affirmations like a mantra; it requires genuine belief and conviction. We must truly believe in the power of our words to influence our reality, and we must align our thoughts, words, and actions accordingly.

In the words of Napoleon Hill, "Whatever the mind can conceive and believe, it can achieve." Auto-suggestion is the bridge that connects our conscious desires with our subconscious mind, enabling us to tap into its vast reservoir of creative potential. By harnessing the power of auto-suggestion, we can unleash the full power of our subconscious mind and create the life of our dreams.

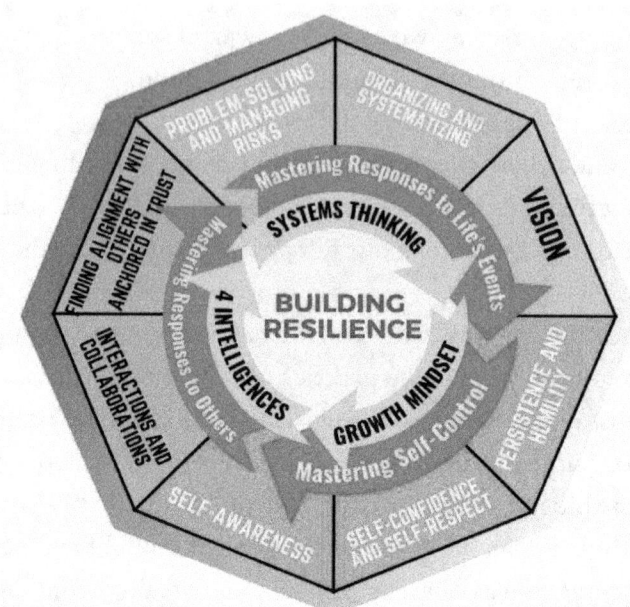

BUILDING RESILIENCE OCTAGON FRAMEWORK

35

Specialized Knowledge: Personalizing Your Path to Success

Specialized knowledge is the cornerstone of success, providing individuals with a unique advantage in their chosen field or endeavor. It is not just about acquiring general information, but rather about delving deep into a specific area of expertise and becoming a master in that domain.

In today's complex and competitive world, having specialized knowledge sets individuals apart from the crowd. It enables them to offer unique insights, solve complex problems, and deliver exceptional value to their clients, customers, or employers.

But specialized knowledge is not just about acquiring qualifications or degrees; it is about a lifelong commitment to learning and growth. It requires continuous study, practice, and refinement, as well as a willingness to adapt to changing circumstances and emerging trends.

By personalizing our path to success through specialized knowledge, we are able to carve out our own niche in the world. We become experts in our chosen field, respected authorities whose opinions are sought after and valued by others.

Moreover, specialized knowledge empowers us to create opportunities where others see only obstacles. It enables us to identify unmet needs, untapped markets, and innovative solutions that can propel us to new heights of success.

In the words of Napoleon Hill, "Knowledge is only potential power until it is organized into definite plans of action." Specialized knowledge provides us with the tools and insights we need to formulate clear and actionable plans for achieving our goals.

Ultimately, specialized knowledge is not just about personal success; it is about making a meaningful impact on the world around us. By leveraging our unique talents and expertise, we can contribute to the greater good and leave a lasting legacy that inspires others to follow in our footsteps.

Specialized knowledge is the cornerstone of achievement and success. It refers to expertise in a particular field or domain, acquired through education, training, and experience. In a world filled with endless opportunities, possessing specialized knowledge gives individuals a competitive edge and opens doors to new possibilities.

Unlike general knowledge, which is widely accessible and often superficial, specialized knowledge is deep, focused, and highly valuable. It allows individuals to become masters of their craft, to excel in their chosen profession, and to make unique contributions to their field.

Personalizing your path to success involves identifying your passions, interests, and strengths, and then acquiring specialized knowledge in areas that align with these factors. By doing so, you not only increase your expertise and credibility but also create opportunities for yourself that others may overlook.

Specialized knowledge empowers individuals to solve complex problems, innovate new solutions, and create value in ways that are uniquely their own. It gives them the confidence to pursue their goals with clarity and conviction, knowing that they have the skills and expertise necessary to succeed.

But acquiring specialized knowledge is not always easy. It requires dedication, commitment, and a willingness to continually learn and adapt. It may involve investing time and resources in formal education, training programs, or hands-on experience.

However, the rewards of specialized knowledge are well worth the effort.

SPECIALIZED KNOWLEDGE: PERSONALIZING YOUR PATH TO SUCCESS

It opens doors to new opportunities, enhances career prospects, and enriches lives in ways that extend far beyond financial gain. Whether you're an entrepreneur, a professional, or an aspiring leader, specialized knowledge is the key to unlocking your full potential and personalizing your path to success.

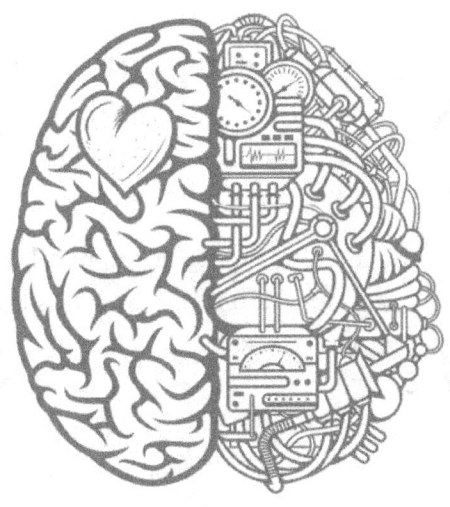

36

36

Imagination: The Workshop of the Mind

Imagination is the creative engine of the mind, the workshop where ideas are born and innovation flourishes. It is the faculty that allows us to visualize new possibilities, dream of better futures, and conceive solutions to challenges.

Imagination is not limited by the constraints of reality; it transcends the physical world and taps into the infinite realm of possibilities. It allows us to envision what could be, rather than being confined to what is. This ability to think beyond the present and explore new horizons is what drives progress and transformation.

In the realm of imagination, there are no boundaries. We can create and manipulate scenarios, design new inventions, and conceptualize groundbreaking ideas. It is through the power of imagination that great artists create masterpieces, inventors develop revolutionary technologies, and entrepreneurs build innovative businesses.

Imagination also plays a crucial role in problem-solving. By visualizing different outcomes and experimenting with various approaches in our minds, we can identify the best course of action. This mental rehearsal helps us prepare for real-life challenges and enhances our ability to navigate complex situations.

Moreover, imagination fuels motivation and inspires us to pursue our goals with passion and determination. When we can clearly see the end result of our efforts in our minds, we are more likely to stay committed and overcome obstacles along the way.

Napoleon Hill described imagination as "the workshop of the mind," emphasizing its role in transforming ideas into reality. By harnessing the power of imagination, we can turn abstract concepts into tangible achievements and bring our dreams to life.

Cultivating imagination requires us to remain curious, open-minded, and willing to explore new perspectives. It involves nurturing our creativity through continuous learning, experimentation, and reflection.

In essence, imagination is the driving force behind innovation and success. It is the workshop of the mind where the seeds of greatness are sown, nurtured, and brought to fruition. By embracing and honing our imaginative abilities, we unlock our potential to achieve extraordinary things and shape a brighter future.

Imagination is the creative engine of the mind, the workshop where dreams are conceived and plans are forged. It is the faculty that enables us to envision possibilities beyond our current reality and to transform abstract ideas into concrete achievements.

Imagination is not just the realm of artists and inventors; it is a vital tool for anyone seeking to achieve success. It allows us to see opportunities where others see obstacles, to innovate new solutions, and to craft compelling visions of the future.

There are two forms of imagination: synthetic imagination and creative imagination. Synthetic imagination involves rearranging existing ideas, concepts, and experiences into new combinations. It is the process of building upon what is already known to create something novel and useful. Creative imagination, on the other hand, is the ability to generate entirely new ideas and concepts that transcend the boundaries of current knowledge and experience. It taps into the subconscious mind, drawing inspiration from the infinite reservoir of universal intelligence.

To harness the power of imagination, it is essential to cultivate a mindset of curiosity and open-mindedness. This involves questioning assumptions, exploring new perspectives, and embracing the unknown. By doing so, we create fertile ground for innovative ideas to take root and flourish.

Imagination is also closely linked to visualization. By vividly picturing our goals and desires in our minds, we can bring them closer to reality. Visualization helps to clarify our intentions, strengthen our belief in our ability to achieve them, and guide our actions towards their fulfillment.

In the words of Napoleon Hill, "Whatever the mind can conceive and believe, it can achieve." Imagination is the tool that allows us to conceive our dreams and to shape our destiny. It is the workshop of the mind, where the seeds of success are sown and nurtured until they blossom into reality. By harnessing the power of imagination, we unlock the full potential of our creativity and pave the way for extraordinary achievements.

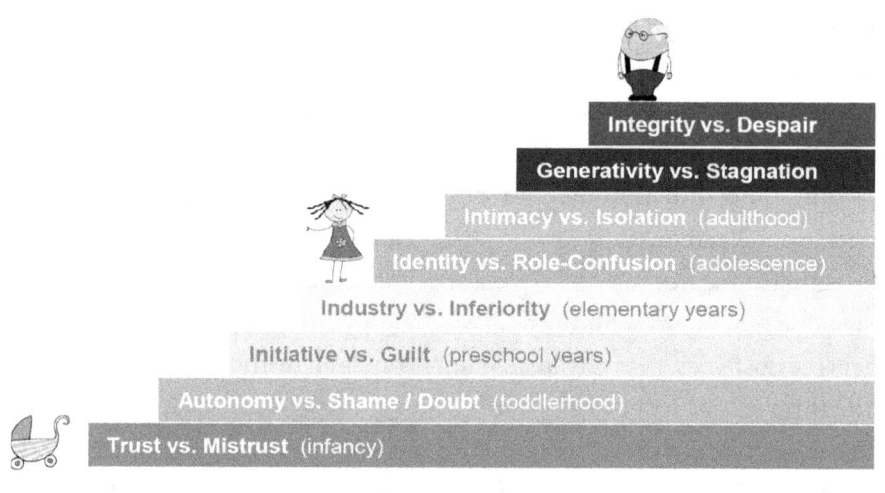

37

37

Organized Planning: Turning Your Ideas into Action Plans

Organized planning is the bridge between dreams and reality, the process through which ideas are transformed into actionable steps. It is the systematic approach to achieving your goals by devising detailed and coherent plans that guide your efforts and resources towards desired outcomes.

The foundation of organized planning begins with setting clear and specific goals. Knowing precisely what you want to achieve allows you to create a roadmap for how to get there. Vague aspirations must be turned into concrete objectives, which are measurable and time-bound.

Once your goals are defined, the next step is to break them down into smaller, manageable tasks. This process, known as task decomposition, helps to identify the steps needed to reach your goals. Each task should have a specific purpose, timeline, and responsible person if you're working with a team.

Effective planning also requires prioritization. Not all tasks are equally important, and some may need to be completed before others can begin. By prioritizing tasks, you ensure that you are focusing your energy and resources on the most critical activities that will drive progress.

Another key component of organized planning is resource allocation. This involves identifying the resources you will need to complete your tasks, including time, money, tools, and personnel. Proper resource management ensures that you have what you need when you need it, and helps to avoid bottlenecks and delays.

Flexibility is also essential in organized planning. While it's important to have a structured plan, it's equally important to remain adaptable and open to adjustments. Unforeseen challenges and opportunities may arise, and being able to pivot and adjust your plan accordingly can be the difference between success and failure.

Execution is where plans come to life. Consistent and disciplined action is crucial. Regularly reviewing your progress against your plan helps to keep you on track and allows for timely adjustments. This iterative process ensures that you are continuously moving towards your goals, learning from experience, and refining your approach.

In the words of Napoleon Hill, "Plan your work and work your plan." Organized planning is not just about creating a plan; it's about committing to a process of continual improvement and disciplined execution. By turning your ideas into actionable steps, you transform aspirations into achievements and pave the way for sustained success.

Organized planning is the bridge that connects your dreams and ideas to tangible achievements. It involves systematically arranging your goals and the steps needed to achieve them, ensuring that every action you take moves you closer to success.

Ideas, no matter how brilliant, remain mere fantasies without a concrete plan to bring them to life. Organized planning transforms these ideas into actionable plans by breaking down the journey into manageable steps. This process involves setting clear objectives, identifying resources, allocating time effectively, and anticipating potential obstacles.

The first step in organized planning is to define your goal clearly. What exactly do you want to achieve? Be specific and set measurable milestones. This clarity will provide direction and help you stay focused on your end objective.

Next, conduct a thorough analysis of your current situation. Assess your

ORGANIZED PLANNING: TURNING YOUR IDEAS INTO ACTION PLANS

strengths, weaknesses, opportunities, and threats (SWOT analysis). This will help you understand what resources you have at your disposal and what challenges you might face. Use this information to inform your planning process, leveraging your strengths and addressing your weaknesses.

After understanding your starting point, break down your goal into smaller, actionable tasks. Create a step-by-step roadmap that outlines what needs to be done, by whom, and by when. This detailed plan should include short-term and long-term actions, ensuring that you maintain momentum while also keeping an eye on the bigger picture.

Effective planning also involves anticipating obstacles and planning for contingencies. Identify potential risks and develop strategies to mitigate them. This proactive approach will help you stay resilient and adaptable in the face of unexpected challenges.

Time management is another critical aspect of organized planning. Allocate your time wisely, prioritizing tasks based on their importance and urgency. Use tools such as calendars, to-do lists, and project management software to stay organized and track your progress.

Finally, regularly review and adjust your plan as needed. Stay flexible and open to making changes based on new information or changing circumstances. Regularly evaluating your progress ensures that you remain on track and can make informed decisions to keep moving forward.

In the words of Napoleon Hill, "Plan your work and work your plan." Organized planning is the systematic approach that turns your ideas into actionable steps, paving the way for success. By carefully crafting and diligently executing your plans, you can transform your dreams into reality and achieve your desired outcomes.

THE POWER

38

38

Decision: The Mastery of Procrastination

Decision-making is a critical skill that separates successful individuals from those who struggle to achieve their goals. Mastering the art of decision-making involves overcoming procrastination and taking decisive action when needed. Procrastination is often a significant barrier to success, as it delays progress and diminishes momentum. To achieve success, one must learn to make decisions swiftly and confidently.

Indecision is a major obstacle to personal and professional growth. It leads to missed opportunities, wasted time, and increased stress. On the other hand, decisive action propels you forward, opening doors to new possibilities and allowing you to capitalize on opportunities as they arise.

To master procrastination and enhance your decision-making abilities, consider the following strategies:

1. **Cultivate Self-Discipline:** Developing self-discipline is essential for making timely decisions. Set clear goals and establish routines that encourage consistent progress. By holding yourself accountable and maintaining a disciplined approach, you can reduce the tendency to procrastinate.
2. **Embrace Imperfection:** Recognize that no decision is ever perfect. Waiting for the "perfect" moment or the "perfect" information often leads

to inaction. Instead, focus on making informed decisions based on the best available information and be prepared to adapt as new information emerges.
3. **Set Deadlines:** Deadlines create a sense of urgency and motivate action. Establish specific timeframes for making decisions and stick to them. This practice helps to eliminate the endless deliberation that often accompanies procrastination.
4. **Prioritize Decisions:** Not all decisions carry the same weight. Identify which decisions are most critical to your goals and prioritize them. Tackle high-priority decisions first, and address less critical ones as time allows.
5. **Break Down Decisions:** Large, complex decisions can be overwhelming and lead to procrastination. Break them down into smaller, manageable steps. This approach makes the decision-making process more approachable and reduces the tendency to delay action.
6. **Seek Feedback:** Don't be afraid to seek input from trusted colleagues, mentors, or friends. Their perspectives can provide valuable insights and help you make more informed decisions. However, avoid becoming overly reliant on others' opinions; trust your judgment and take responsibility for your choices.
7. **Reflect and Learn:** After making a decision, take time to reflect on the outcome. Analyze what worked well and what could be improved. This reflection will enhance your decision-making skills over time and build confidence in your ability to make sound choices.

In the words of Napoleon Hill, "Successful people make decisions quickly (as soon as all the facts are available) and change them slowly, if ever." By mastering the art of decision-making and overcoming procrastination, you can take control of your destiny and achieve your goals with greater efficiency and confidence. Remember, the power to change your life lies in the decisions you make today.

Decision-making is a critical skill that can determine the trajectory of your success. It is the antidote to procrastination, enabling you to take decisive action rather than being paralyzed by indecision and delay. Mastering the art of decision-making empowers you to seize opportunities, overcome obstacles, and move steadily toward your goals.

Procrastination often stems from fear—fear of failure, fear of making the wrong choice, or fear of the unknown. This fear can lead to a state of inaction, where opportunities are missed, and progress is stalled. The key to overcoming procrastination is to develop the habit of making firm, confident decisions.

The first step in mastering decision-making is to cultivate a mindset of clarity and focus. Define your goals clearly and understand why they are important to you. This clarity provides a strong foundation for making decisions that align with your long-term objectives.

Next, gather relevant information and consider your options. Evaluate the potential risks and benefits of each choice, but avoid getting bogged down in excessive analysis. While it's important to be informed, overanalyzing can lead to analysis paralysis, where you become so overwhelmed by data that you fail to make any decision at all.

Trust your instincts and intuition. While logical analysis is essential, your gut feelings often reflect your subconscious mind's deep understanding of a situation. Balancing logic with intuition can lead to more well-rounded and effective decisions.

Set deadlines for your decisions. Giving yourself a specific timeframe to make a choice prevents endless deliberation and forces you to commit to a course of action. Remember, a good decision made promptly is often better than a perfect decision made too late.

Once you've made a decision, take immediate action. Procrastination thrives in the gap between deciding and doing. By acting quickly, you build momentum and create a sense of accomplishment that propels you forward.

It's also important to recognize that not all decisions will be perfect, and mistakes are a natural part of the learning process. Instead of fearing failure, view it as an opportunity to learn and grow. Adjust your course as needed, but keep moving forward with determination.

In the words of Napoleon Hill, "Indecision is the seedling of fear." By mastering the art of decision-making, you can conquer procrastination and take control of your destiny. Decisions are the stepping stones on the path to success, and each one brings you closer to your goals. Embrace the power of decisive action, and you will find that the mastery of procrastination is within your reach.

39

39

Persistence: The Sustained Effort Necessary to Induce Faith

Persistence is the backbone of success, the sustained effort that keeps us moving forward even when faced with challenges and setbacks. It is the quality that distinguishes those who achieve their dreams from those who give up too soon. Persistence is not just about sheer determination; it is about maintaining faith in our goals and ourselves, even when the journey gets tough.

To induce faith, persistence must be unwavering. Faith is built through repeated actions and consistent effort. When we persist, we demonstrate our commitment to our goals, reinforcing our belief that success is possible. This sustained effort cultivates an inner confidence and trust in our abilities.

Persistence begins with a clear and compelling vision of what we want to achieve. This vision acts as our guiding star, keeping us focused and motivated. With a strong vision in mind, we can overcome temporary obstacles and maintain our course.

The path to success is rarely a straight line. It is filled with detours, obstacles, and moments of doubt. During these times, persistence is our greatest ally. By refusing to give up, we build resilience and adaptability, learning valuable lessons from each setback. These experiences strengthen our resolve and enhance our ability to overcome future challenges.

One of the most important aspects of persistence is maintaining a positive mindset. Challenges and failures are inevitable, but how we respond to them makes all the difference. A positive attitude helps us see setbacks as opportunities for growth rather than insurmountable barriers. By focusing on solutions rather than problems, we can maintain our momentum and continue moving forward.

Persistence also involves setting realistic and achievable goals. Break down your larger vision into smaller, manageable tasks. Celebrate each small victory along the way, as these achievements fuel your motivation and reinforce your belief in your ultimate success.

Surround yourself with supportive people who believe in your vision and encourage your efforts. A strong support network can provide invaluable encouragement and perspective, helping you stay persistent during tough times.

In the words of Napoleon Hill, "Victory is always possible for the person who refuses to stop fighting." Persistence is the sustained effort that nurtures our faith and propels us toward our goals. It is the unwavering commitment to keep going, no matter how difficult the journey may be. By embracing persistence, we develop the strength and resilience necessary to achieve our dreams and create the life we desire.

Persistence is the unwavering commitment to your goals, the relentless drive that propels you forward even in the face of obstacles and setbacks. It is the sustained effort that breathes life into your dreams and turns aspirations into achievements. Without persistence, even the most compelling vision can wither away before it comes to fruition.

The journey to success is rarely a straight path. It is often filled with challenges, disappointments, and moments of doubt. Persistence is what keeps you moving forward, helping you to overcome these hurdles and stay on course. It is the ability to maintain your focus and continue striving towards your goals, no matter how difficult the circumstances.

Persistence is closely linked to faith—the belief in your ability to achieve your goals. When you persist, you reinforce your faith in your vision and in yourself. Each small victory, each step forward, strengthens your confidence

PERSISTENCE: THE SUSTAINED EFFORT NECESSARY TO INDUCE FAITH

and solidifies your commitment. Over time, this sustained effort builds an unshakeable faith that propels you toward success.

Developing persistence requires a clear understanding of your goals and a deep-seated desire to achieve them. This clarity of purpose fuels your determination and gives you the resilience to keep going when the going gets tough. Set specific, measurable, and achievable goals to give your persistence a clear direction.

Another key to persistence is cultivating a positive mindset. Embrace challenges as opportunities for growth and learning. Instead of seeing setbacks as failures, view them as valuable experiences that bring you closer to your goal. Maintaining a positive outlook helps you stay motivated and focused, even in difficult times.

Persistence also involves discipline and consistency. Make a habit of working towards your goals every day, no matter how small the steps may seem. Consistent effort, over time, leads to significant progress. Establish routines and practices that support your goals, and stick to them with unwavering dedication.

Surround yourself with supportive and like-minded individuals who encourage and inspire you. A strong support network can provide motivation, advice, and encouragement when you need it most. Seek out mentors, peers, and communities that share your values and aspirations.

Finally, be patient and trust the process. Success often takes time, and the road to achievement is seldom quick or easy. Understand that persistence is a long-term commitment, and stay focused on your vision, even when progress seems slow.

In the words of Napoleon Hill, "Victory is always possible for the person who refuses to stop fighting." Persistence is the sustained effort that induces faith, the relentless pursuit of your dreams despite the challenges you face. By cultivating persistence, you harness the power to achieve your goals and realize your fullest potential. Keep pressing forward, and you will find that success is not just a possibility, but an inevitability.

PERSISTENCE: THE SUSTAINED EFFORT NECESSARY TO INDUCE FAITH

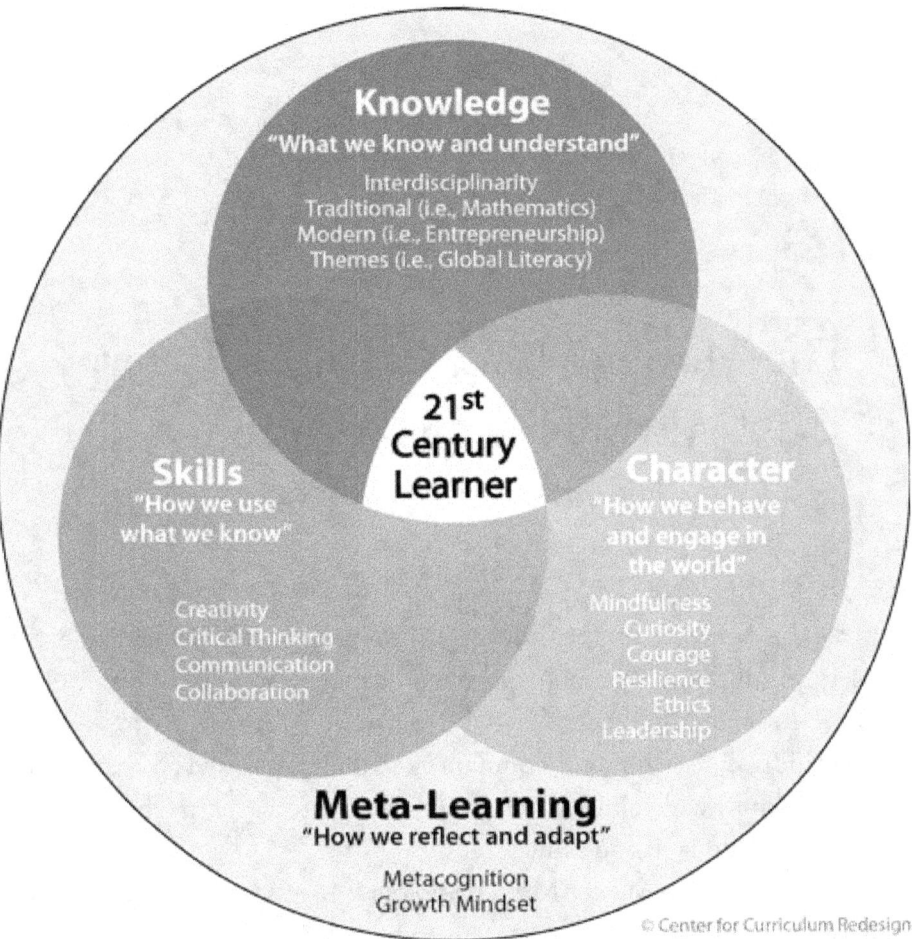

40

40

The Master Mind: Creating Synergy through Collaboration

The concept of the Master Mind is a powerful principle that emphasizes the importance of collaboration and collective effort in achieving success. It involves bringing together a group of like-minded individuals who share common goals and values, and leveraging their combined knowledge, skills, and resources to create a synergy that surpasses what any individual could achieve alone.

At the heart of the Master Mind principle is the idea that the interaction between multiple minds generates an energy and creativity that is greater than the sum of its parts. This synergy is the result of diverse perspectives, ideas, and experiences coming together to solve problems, innovate, and drive progress.

Creating a MasterMind group begins with assembling a team of individuals who possess complementary skills and a shared commitment to mutual success. These members should be chosen not only for their expertise and abilities but also for their willingness to support and challenge each other in a positive and constructive manner.

Effective communication is crucial to the success of a Master Mind group. Open, honest, and respectful dialogue fosters an environment where ideas can be freely exchanged, and constructive criticism can be offered without fear of judgment. This collaborative atmosphere encourages creativity and innovation, leading to breakthroughs that might not have been possible in isolation.

Trust and mutual respect are foundational elements of any successful Master Mind group. Members must feel confident in sharing their thoughts and ideas, knowing that they will be met with support and encouragement. Building this trust requires consistent, reliable behavior and a genuine commitment to the success of the group as a whole.

Regular meetings and structured agendas help maintain focus and ensure that the group stays on track towards its goals. These meetings provide opportunities for brainstorming, problem-solving, and strategic planning, as well as for celebrating successes and learning from setbacks.

The Master Mind principle also highlights the importance of accountability. Members hold each other accountable for their commitments and actions, providing motivation and encouragement to stay on course. This accountability helps ensure that everyone remains aligned with the group's objectives and continues to contribute effectively.

Napoleon Hill, the proponent of the Master Mind concept, stated, "No two minds ever come together without thereby creating a third, invisible, intangible force, which may be likened to a third mind." This "third mind" is the collective intelligence and creative power that emerges from effective collaboration, driving the group towards greater achievements.

In summary, the Master Mind principle is about harnessing the power of collaboration to create synergy and achieve extraordinary results. By bringing together individuals with diverse skills and a shared vision, fostering open communication and trust, and maintaining accountability and focus, a MasterMind group can unlock new levels of creativity and success. Embrace the power of the Master Mind, and you will find that together, you can achieve more than you ever could alone.

The concept of the Master Mind emphasizes the power of collaboration and collective intelligence. It involves bringing together a group of like-minded individuals who share common goals and values, pooling their knowledge, skills, and experiences to create synergy. This collective effort results in outcomes that are far greater than what any individual could achieve alone.

A Master Mind group harnesses the principle that the whole is greater than the sum of its parts. When people come together to collaborate, they can generate innovative ideas, solve complex problems, and support each other in ways that are impossible individually. The exchange of diverse perspectives and expertise enriches the decision-making process, leading to more effective strategies and solutions.

To form a successful Master Mind group, it is essential to select members carefully. Choose individuals who are not only knowledgeable and skilled but also committed to mutual success and personal growth. The ideal group members should have a shared vision and be willing to contribute their time, energy, and resources to support each other's goals.

Effective communication is the cornerstone of a successful Master Mind group. Establish open, honest, and respectful channels of communication where members feel comfortable sharing their ideas, challenges, and insights. Regular meetings, whether in person or virtual, help to maintain focus, accountability, and momentum.

In a Master Mind group, each member plays a dual role as both a teacher and a learner. By sharing their unique experiences and expertise, members can provide valuable guidance and support to their peers. At the same time, they can learn from the insights and feedback of others, enhancing their own knowledge and capabilities.

The power of the Master Mind lies in its ability to amplify the potential of each member. Collaboration fosters creativity and innovation, as diverse perspectives lead to new ideas and approaches. Additionally, the collective support and encouragement from the group can boost individual motivation and confidence, helping members to overcome obstacles and stay committed to their goals.

Accountability is another key benefit of a Master Mind group. When members commit to specific actions and deadlines, the group holds them accountable, providing a powerful incentive to follow through on their commitments. This accountability helps to maintain focus and discipline, ensuring steady progress towards goals.

THE MASTER MIND: CREATING SYNERGY THROUGH COLLABORATION

In the words of Napoleon Hill, "No two minds ever come together without thereby creating a third, invisible, intangible force, which may be likened to a third mind." This "third mind" is the synergistic power of the Master Mind, a force that can unlock new levels of achievement and success.

Creating synergy through collaboration in a Master Mind group is a powerful strategy for personal and professional growth. By leveraging the collective intelligence and support of a dedicated group, you can achieve extraordinary results and reach your highest potential. Embrace the power of the Master Mind, and discover the limitless possibilities that arise when minds come together in pursuit of a common goal.

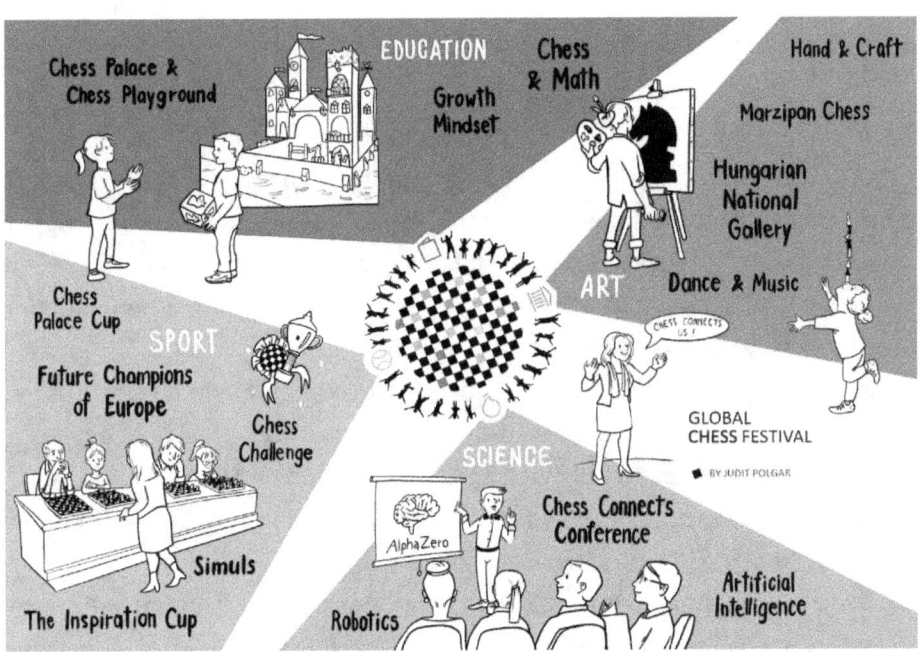

41

41

The Mystery of Sex Transmutation: Harnessing Creative Energy

Sex transmutation is a concept that explores the transformative power of redirecting sexual energy towards creative endeavors and higher pursuits. It suggests that the energy generated by sexual desire, when channeled and sublimated, can be converted into a potent force for creativity, productivity, and personal growth.

Sexual energy is one of the most powerful forces in human nature, driving our desires, motivations, and actions. When left unchecked or misdirected, it can lead to distraction, impulsivity, and even destructive behaviors. However, when harnessed and channeled effectively, this same energy can fuel our creativity, innovation, and drive for success.

The key to sex transmutation lies in consciously redirecting sexual energy towards constructive and productive activities. Rather than dissipating this energy through purely physical or fleeting pursuits, individuals can channel it into creative endeavors, intellectual pursuits, or personal development activities.

One way to harness sexual energy is through creative expression. Many artists, writers, and musicians throughout history have credited their most inspired works to moments of heightened sexual energy. By channeling this energy into their creative process, they are able to tap into a deep well of inspiration and produce work that is both powerful and impactful.

Another approach to sex transmutation is through intellectual pursuits and self-improvement activities. By focusing their energy on learning, growth, and personal development, individuals can channel their sexual energy towards achieving their goals and realizing their fullest potential. This can manifest in increased focus, motivation, and drive to succeed in various aspects of life.

Spiritual practices also offer techniques for harnessing sexual energy for personal transformation and enlightenment. Practices such as meditation, yoga, and tantra teach individuals to cultivate awareness and mastery over their sexual energy, allowing them to tap into its immense power for spiritual growth and awakening.

Ultimately, sex transmutation is about harnessing the raw power of sexual energy and channeling it towards higher purposes. By recognizing the potential of this energy and learning to control and direct it effectively, individuals can unlock new levels of creativity, productivity, and fulfillment in their lives.

In the words of Napoleon Hill, "Sex desire is the most powerful of human desires. When driven by this desire, men develop keenness of imagination, courage, will-power, persistence, and creative ability unknown to them at other times." By mastering the mystery of sex transmutation, individuals can tap into this powerful force and unleash their full creative potential.

The subconscious mind is a vast reservoir of untapped potential within each of us, holding the key to unlocking our inner power and shaping our reality. It operates beneath the surface of our conscious awareness, influencing our thoughts, feelings, and behaviors in profound ways.

Understanding and harnessing the power of the subconscious mind is essential for personal growth and self-improvement. It is the seat of our beliefs, attitudes, and habits, shaping our perceptions of the world and guiding our actions. By connecting with our subconscious, we can uncover hidden patterns, overcome limiting beliefs, and unleash our full potential.

One of the most effective ways to access the power of the subconscious mind is through techniques such as visualization, affirmation, and meditation.

By engaging in these practices regularly, we can reprogram our subconscious with positive beliefs and intentions, aligning ourselves with our deepest desires and aspirations.

Visualization involves mentally picturing our goals and desires as if they have already been achieved. By vividly imagining our desired outcomes, we imprint them onto our subconscious mind, which then works to manifest them in our reality. Affirmations are positive statements that we repeat to ourselves regularly, reinforcing empowering beliefs and attitudes. Through repetition, affirmations penetrate the subconscious mind, replacing negative self-talk with confidence and optimism.

Meditation is another powerful tool for accessing the subconscious mind. By quieting the conscious chatter of the mind and entering a state of deep relaxation, we can bypass the critical faculties and connect with our inner wisdom. In this state, we can access insights, inspiration, and guidance that can help us navigate life's challenges and make informed decisions.

Developing a deeper awareness of our subconscious mind also involves paying attention to our dreams, intuition, and gut instincts. These subtle signals often contain valuable information and guidance from our inner selves. By listening to our intuition and trusting our inner guidance, we can tap into the limitless wisdom and power of the subconscious mind.

In the words of Napoleon Hill, "What the mind can conceive and believe, it can achieve." By connecting with our subconscious mind and aligning ourselves with our deepest desires, we can unlock our inner power and create the life of our dreams. Through regular practice and mindfulness, we can harness the transformative potential of the subconscious mind and unleash our full creative potential.

THE MYSTERY OF SEX TRANSMUTATION: HARNESSING CREATIVE ENERGY

42

42

The Subconscious Mind: Connecting with Your Inner Power

The subconscious mind is a vast reservoir of untapped potential within each of us, holding the key to unlocking our inner power and shaping our reality. It operates beneath the surface of our conscious awareness, influencing our thoughts, feelings, and behaviors in profound ways.

Understanding and harnessing the power of the subconscious mind is essential for personal growth and self-improvement. It is the seat of our beliefs, attitudes, and habits, shaping our perceptions of the world and guiding our actions. By connecting with our subconscious, we can uncover hidden patterns, overcome limiting beliefs, and unleash our full potential.

One of the most effective ways to access the power of the subconscious mind is through techniques such as visualization, affirmation, and meditation. By engaging in these practices regularly, we can reprogram our subconscious with positive beliefs and intentions, aligning ourselves with our deepest desires and aspirations.

Visualization involves mentally picturing our goals and desires as if they have already been achieved. By vividly imagining our desired outcomes, we imprint them onto our subconscious mind, which then works to manifest them in our reality. Affirmations are positive statements that we repeat to ourselves regularly, reinforcing empowering beliefs and attitudes. Through repetition, affirmations penetrate the subconscious mind, replacing negative self-talk with confidence and optimism.

Meditation is another powerful tool for accessing the subconscious mind. By quieting the conscious chatter of the mind and entering a state of deep relaxation, we can bypass the critical faculties and connect with our inner wisdom. In this state, we can access insights, inspiration, and guidance that can help us navigate life's challenges and make informed decisions.

Developing a deeper awareness of our subconscious mind also involves paying attention to our dreams, intuition, and gut instincts. These subtle signals often contain valuable information and guidance from our inner selves. By listening to our intuition and trusting our inner guidance, we can tap into the limitless wisdom and power of the subconscious mind.

In the words of Napoleon Hill, "What the mind can conceive and believe, it can achieve." By connecting with our subconscious mind and aligning ourselves with our deepest desires, we can unlock our inner power and create the life of our dreams. Through regular practice and mindfulness, we can harness the transformative potential of the subconscious mind and unleash our full creative potential.

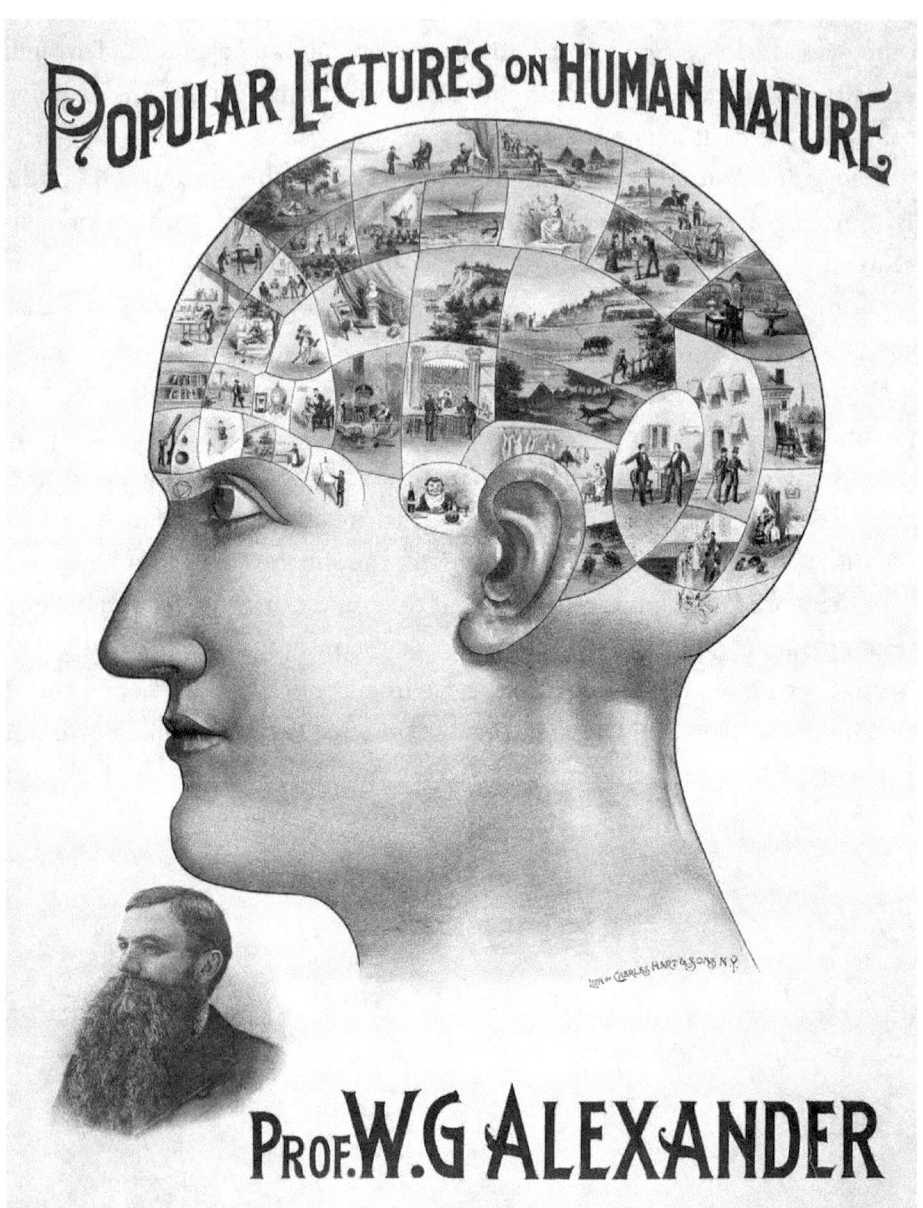

43

43

The Brain: A Broadcasting and Receiving Station for Thought

The human brain is an extraordinary organ with capabilities far beyond what we often realize. It serves as both a broadcasting and receiving station for thought, constantly sending and receiving signals that shape our perceptions, emotions, and actions.

At its core, the brain is a complex network of neurons and synapses that communicate through electrical impulses. These impulses create patterns of activity that give rise to our thoughts, memories, and consciousness. But the brain's functions extend far beyond mere processing; it also acts as a transmitter and receiver of thought energy.

Our thoughts are not confined to the confines of our skulls; they have the power to extend beyond our physical bodies and influence the world around us. Just as a radio station broadcasts signals that can be picked up by receivers, our brains emit thought vibrations that can be detected by others, whether consciously or unconsciously.

Similarly, we are constantly receiving thought energy from the world around us. We are bombarded with a constant stream of information, opinions, and ideas from our environment, which can shape our beliefs, attitudes, and behaviors. Like tuning into different radio stations, we can choose which thoughts to focus on and which to ignore.

The concept of the brain as a broadcasting and receiving station for thought has profound implications for personal development and self-awareness. By becoming more conscious of the thoughts we emit and the ones we allow ourselves to absorb, we can take greater control over our mental and emotional well-being.

Positive thinking, visualization, and affirmations are powerful tools for harnessing the broadcasting capabilities of the brain. By consciously directing our thoughts towards positive outcomes and desired goals, we can amplify their energetic vibrations and increase the likelihood of manifesting them in our reality.

Likewise, mindfulness and meditation help to quiet the mental chatter and attune our minds to the subtle signals of intuition and inner wisdom. By creating space for silence and stillness, we open ourselves up to receiving guidance and inspiration from the universal consciousness.

In the words of Napoleon Hill, "Truly, 'thoughts are things,' and powerful things at that." By understanding and harnessing the broadcasting and receiving capabilities of the brain, we can tap into the infinite potential of thought energy and create the life we desire. Through awareness, intention, and practice, we can elevate our consciousness and harness the transformative power of thought.

The human brain is an extraordinary organ, serving as both a broadcasting and receiving station for thought. It acts as a powerful transmitter and receiver, constantly sending and receiving signals that shape our perceptions, beliefs, and experiences.

At its core, the brain functions as a sophisticated information-processing system, capable of processing vast amounts of data and stimuli from both internal and external sources. It interprets sensory input, analyzes information, and generates responses based on past experiences, learned patterns, and biological instincts.

But the brain is more than just a passive processor of information; it is also a dynamic generator of thought. It has the remarkable ability to create, store, and retrieve memories, thoughts, and ideas. Through the complex interactions of neurons and neurotransmitters, the brain generates electrical

THE BRAIN: A BROADCASTING AND RECEIVING STATION FOR THOUGHT

impulses that give rise to conscious thought and awareness.

One of the most fascinating aspects of the brain is its role in shaping our reality through the power of thought. Our thoughts have a profound influence on our emotions, behaviors, and experiences. They can shape our perceptions of the world, influence our beliefs and attitudes, and even impact our physical health and well-being.

The brain acts as a broadcasting station for our thoughts, sending out energetic signals that can attract or repel people, opportunities, and circumstances into our lives. Positive thoughts emit vibrations of optimism, hope, and abundance, drawing similar energies towards us. Conversely, negative thoughts radiate frequencies of fear, doubt, and scarcity, repelling positive outcomes and opportunities.

But the brain is also a receiving station for thought, picking up on the energetic vibrations and frequencies emitted by others. It is highly attuned to nonverbal cues, body language, and subtle energetic signals, allowing us to intuitively sense the thoughts and intentions of those around us.

By understanding the power of the brain as a broadcasting and receiving station for thought, we can become more intentional about the thoughts we choose to focus on. We can cultivate a positive mindset, cultivate gratitude, and consciously direct our thoughts towards our goals and aspirations. Through mindfulness, visualization, and positive affirmations, we can harness the creative power of the brain to manifest our deepest desires and create the life we truly want to live.

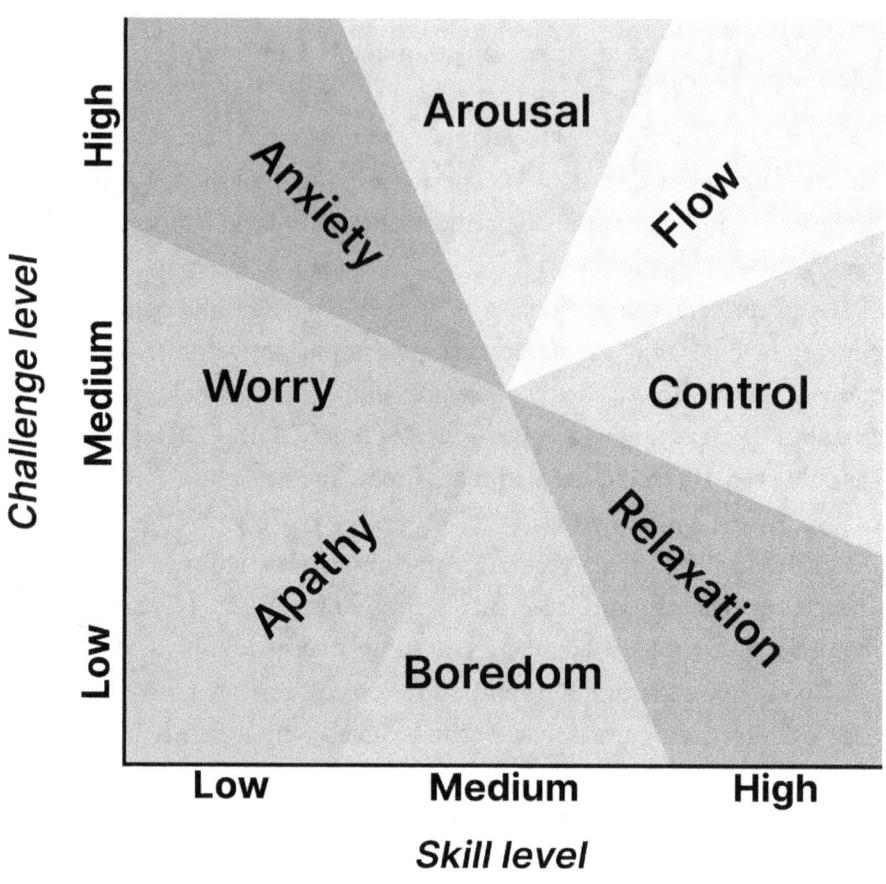

44

The Sixth Sense: The Door to the Temple of Wisdom

The concept of the sixth sense represents an innate faculty of perception that transcends the five physical senses of sight, hearing, touch, taste, and smell. It is often described as intuition, inner knowing, or gut feeling—an intuitive sense of understanding that goes beyond logical reasoning and empirical evidence.

The sixth sense serves as a doorway to the temple of wisdom, granting us access to deeper insights, higher truths, and spiritual awareness. It allows us to tap into the vast reservoir of universal intelligence and connect with the divine wisdom that lies within us and around us.

Unlike the other five senses, which rely on external stimuli to perceive the world, the sixth sense operates on a subtler, more intuitive level. It is the voice of our inner guidance, offering guidance, clarity, and direction in times of uncertainty or doubt.

Developing our sixth sense requires cultivating mindfulness, openness, and receptivity to subtle cues and signals from the universe. It involves quieting the chatter of the mind, tuning into our inner wisdom, and trusting the intuitive nudges and insights that arise.

The sixth sense is not limited to any particular individual or group; it is a universal gift that is available to all who are willing to cultivate it. By honoring our intuition and trusting our inner guidance, we can tap into the infinite wellspring of wisdom that resides within us.

In the words of Napoleon Hill, "Every adversity, every failure, every heartache carries with it the seed of an equal or greater benefit." By developing our sixth sense and accessing the wisdom it offers, we can navigate life's challenges with grace and resilience. We can make decisions that are aligned with our highest good and pursue paths that lead to fulfillment, joy, and spiritual growth.

The sixth sense is not something that can be learned or acquired through external means; it is a natural aspect of our being that is always present, waiting to be acknowledged and embraced. By quieting the mind, tuning into our inner guidance, and trusting the wisdom that arises, we can unlock the door to the temple of wisdom and experience the profound transformation that comes from aligning with our truest selves.

The sixth sense is often regarded as the gateway to a higher level of consciousness and understanding—an intuitive faculty that transcends the five traditional senses of sight, hearing, touch, taste, and smell. It is the inner knowing, the gut feeling, the instinctive awareness that goes beyond rational thought and logical analysis.

While the existence of the sixth sense may seem mysterious or elusive, many cultures and spiritual traditions acknowledge its presence and significance. It is believed to be a natural, innate ability that all human beings possess to varying degrees, although it often remains dormant or undeveloped in many individuals.

The sixth sense operates on a subtle level, communicating through feelings, impressions, and subtle energies. It can manifest as a hunch, a premonition, or a sudden insight that seems to come out of nowhere. It bypasses the limitations of the rational mind, tapping into a deeper well of wisdom and intuition.

Developing and honing the sixth sense requires openness, receptivity, and trust in one's inner guidance. It involves quieting the noise of the external world and tuning into the subtle signals of the inner self. Practices such as meditation, mindfulness, and deep listening can help to cultivate this intuitive

THE SIXTH SENSE: THE DOOR TO THE TEMPLE OF WISDOM

awareness and attunement.

The sixth sense is often associated with creativity, inspiration, and spiritual insight. It is the source of artistic inspiration, scientific breakthroughs, and flashes of genius that seem to arise from the depths of the unconscious mind. By accessing this innate wisdom, individuals can tap into a reservoir of creativity and innovation that transcends conventional thinking.

In the words of Napoleon Hill, "There are no limitations to the mind except those we acknowledge." The sixth sense is the key to unlocking the limitless potential of the mind, opening the door to new realms of perception and understanding. By embracing and cultivating this intuitive faculty, individuals can gain access to a deeper level of wisdom and insight, guiding them on their journey towards self-discovery and enlightenment.

45

45

How to Outwit the Six Ghosts of Fear

Fear can be a paralyzing force, holding us back from pursuing our dreams and living our lives to the fullest. It manifests in various forms, often disguising itself as doubt, insecurity, or anxiety. Napoleon Hill identified six common "ghosts" of fear that haunt the human mind and hinder our progress:

1. Fear of poverty: This fear stems from the belief that there will not be enough resources—money, time, or opportunities—to meet our needs or achieve our goals.
2. Fear of criticism: This fear arises from the concern of what others may think or say about us. It can prevent us from taking risks or expressing our true selves for fear of judgment or rejection.
3. Fear of ill health: This fear revolves around the anxiety of illness, injury, or physical decline. It can lead to hypochondria, obsessive health behaviors, or avoidance of activities perceived as risky.
4. Fear of loss of love: This fear arises from the fear of rejection, abandonment, or loss of affection from loved ones. It can manifest as clinginess, jealousy, or avoidance of intimacy.
5. Fear of old age: This fear stems from the dread of aging and the decline of physical and mental faculties. It can lead to a sense of existential dread or a fixation on youth and appearance.

6. Fear of death: This fear is perhaps the most primal and universal of all fears, stemming from the fear of the unknown and the cessation of existence. It can lead to anxiety, depression, or avoidance of anything associated with mortality.

To outwit these ghosts of fear, it is essential to cultivate courage, resilience, and self-awareness. Here are some strategies to overcome fear and reclaim control of your life:

- Identify your fears: Shine a light on your fears by acknowledging and confronting them head-on. Awareness is the first step towards overcoming fear.
- Challenge your beliefs: Examine the underlying beliefs and assumptions that fuel your fears. Are they based on facts or unfounded assumptions? Challenge irrational thoughts with evidence and logic.
- Take action: Take small, gradual steps towards facing your fears. Each success builds confidence and diminishes the power of fear.
- Practice self-compassion: Be kind and gentle with yourself as you confront your fears. Treat yourself with the same empathy and understanding you would offer to a friend facing similar challenges.
- Seek support: Surround yourself with supportive friends, family, or professionals who can offer encouragement, guidance, and perspective.
- Cultivate resilience: Build resilience by embracing failure as an opportunity for growth, learning from setbacks, and bouncing back stronger than before.

By outwitting the six ghosts of fear, you can reclaim your power, liberate yourself from self-imposed limitations, and unlock your full potential. Remember, courage is not the absence of fear but the willingness to face it head-on and continue moving forward despite it.

Fear is a powerful force that can hold us back from realizing our full potential and achieving our goals. It manifests in many forms, often disguising itself as doubt, uncertainty, or anxiety. Napoleon Hill identified six common "ghosts" of fear that haunt the human mind and sabotage our success. Here's how to outwit them:

1. Fear of Poverty: This fear stems from a scarcity mindset and the belief that there's not enough to go around. To outwit this ghost, cultivate a mindset of abundance and focus on opportunities rather than limitations. Take proactive steps to improve your financial literacy and create multiple streams of income.
2. Fear of Criticism: The fear of being judged or ridiculed by others can paralyze us into inaction. To overcome this fear, focus on your own values and priorities rather than seeking validation from others. Remember that criticism is often a reflection of the critic's insecurities, not your worth or abilities.
3. Fear of Ill Health: This fear arises from the uncertainty and vulnerability of our physical well-being. To outwit it, prioritize self-care and adopt healthy habits that support your overall health and vitality. Focus on what you can control, such as diet, exercise, and stress management, rather than worrying about hypothetical worst-case scenarios.
4. Fear of Loss of Love: This fear revolves around the idea of losing the love and approval of those closest to us. To overcome it, cultivate self-love and self-acceptance, recognizing that your worth is not dependent on external validation. Nurture healthy relationships built on trust, communication, and mutual respect.
5. Fear of Old Age: This fear is rooted in the discomfort of facing our mortality and the inevitable changes that come with aging. To outwit it, embrace the natural process of aging as a journey of growth and wisdom. Focus on living a fulfilling and purposeful life at every stage, rather than dwelling on fears of the future.
6. Fear of Death: The ultimate fear, the fear of death, can overshadow our lives and prevent us from fully embracing the present moment. To overcome it, cultivate a sense of spiritual connection and purpose that transcends the fear of physical death. Focus on living a meaningful life aligned with your values and beliefs, knowing that death is a natural

part of the cycle of life.

By understanding and confronting these six ghosts of fear, we can outwit their influence and reclaim our power to live boldly and authentically. Instead of allowing fear to dictate our choices, we can embrace courage, resilience, and inner strength to pursue our dreams and create the life we truly desire.

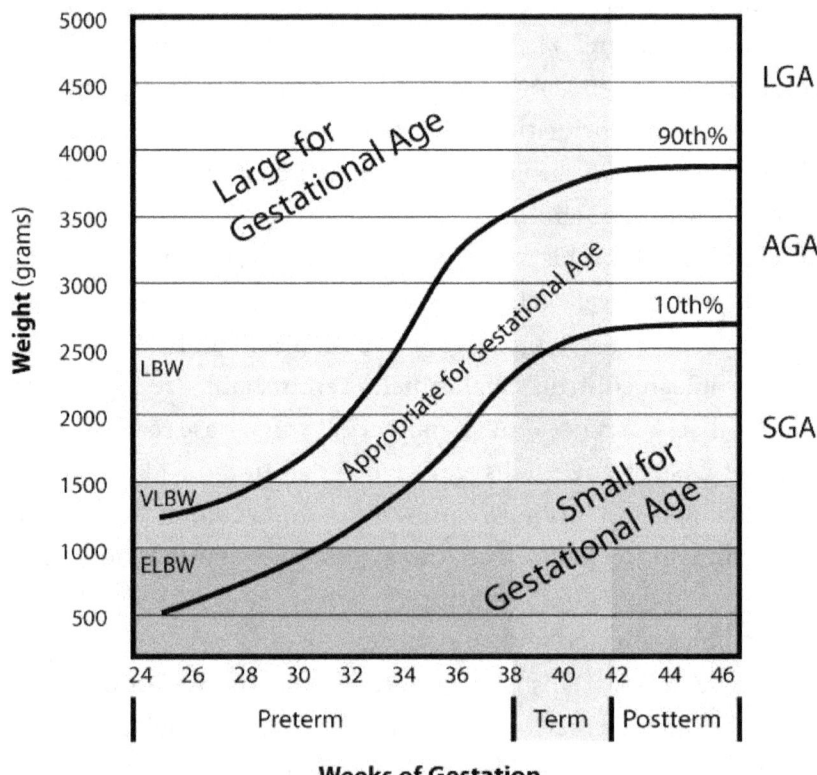

46

The Devil's Workshop: The Power of Negative Thinking

"The Devil's Workshop" is a metaphorical expression used to describe the detrimental effects of negative thinking on our lives. When we allow negative thoughts to take hold in our minds, they can become like a workshop where destructive beliefs and attitudes are manufactured and reinforced.

Negative thinking has a powerful influence on our emotions, behaviors, and outcomes. It can breed feelings of doubt, fear, and insecurity, leading us to second-guess ourselves and sabotage our own success. Like a dark workshop, negative thinking churns out self-limiting beliefs and distorted perceptions that distort our reality and hold us back from reaching our full potential.

The power of negative thinking lies in its ability to shape our experiences and perceptions. When we dwell on negative thoughts, we attract more negativity into our lives, creating a self-perpetuating cycle of despair and defeat. Our minds become consumed by worry, pessimism, and hopelessness, making it difficult to see the possibilities and opportunities that surround us.

To combat the influence of negative thinking, we must become aware of the thoughts and beliefs that are holding us back. We must shine a light into the dark corners of our minds and challenge the validity of negative beliefs.

Are they based on facts and evidence, or are they simply the product of our fears and insecurities?

Once we identify negative thought patterns, we can actively work to replace them with more positive and empowering beliefs. This involves practicing self-awareness and mindfulness, monitoring our thoughts, and consciously choosing to focus on what is good, true, and hopeful. By reframing negative thoughts into more positive perspectives, we can change the way we perceive ourselves and the world around us.

It's important to recognize that overcoming negative thinking is not always easy and may require time, patience, and effort. It's a gradual process of reprogramming our minds and cultivating a more optimistic outlook on life. Surrounding ourselves with positive influences, such as supportive friends, uplifting books, and inspirational role models, can also help to counteract the influence of negativity.

In the words of Napoleon Hill, "Your mental attitude is the most dependable key to your personality." By acknowledging the power of negative thinking and actively working to counteract its influence, we can take control of our minds and create a more positive and fulfilling life for ourselves. Instead of allowing our thoughts to be a devil's workshop, let them become a workshop of possibility, creativity, and growth.

The Devil's Workshop refers to the destructive force of negative thinking, which can undermine our confidence, erode our resilience, and sabotage our success. When we indulge in negative thoughts, we give power to our fears, doubts, and insecurities, creating a breeding ground for unhappiness and self-sabotage.

Negative thinking can take many forms, from self-criticism and self-doubt to catastrophic thinking and pessimism about the future. It can distort our perceptions, magnifying problems and minimizing our strengths and accomplishments. Left unchecked, negative thinking can become a self-perpetuating cycle, reinforcing limiting beliefs and preventing us from realizing our full potential.

The power of negative thinking lies in its ability to shape our reality. When we dwell on negative thoughts, we attract more negativity into our lives, creating a downward spiral of despair and hopelessness. Our thoughts have a profound influence on our emotions, behaviors, and outcomes, shaping our experiences and coloring our perceptions of the world.

To overcome the Devil's Workshop of negative thinking, we must cultivate awareness and vigilance over our thoughts. We must learn to recognize when negative thinking patterns arise and challenge them with positive affirmations, rational thinking, and evidence-based perspectives. Instead of focusing on what could go wrong, we can choose to focus on what we can control and how we can overcome challenges.

Practicing gratitude and mindfulness can also help to counteract negative thinking. By shifting our focus to the present moment and cultivating an attitude of gratitude for the blessings in our lives, we can foster a sense of inner peace and contentment that transcends negativity. Additionally, surrounding ourselves with positive influences and supportive relationships can help to uplift our spirits and reinforce positive thinking patterns.

In the words of Napoleon Hill, "Your mental attitude is the most dependable key to your personality." By cultivating a positive mindset and guarding against the insidious influence of negative thinking, we can reclaim our power to create a life filled with joy, fulfillment, and abundance. Instead of allowing the Devil's Workshop to dictate our thoughts and actions, we can choose to harness the power of positivity and optimism to shape our destiny.

47

47

The Law of Cosmic Habit Force: The Science of Personal Achievement

The Law of Cosmic Habit Force is a principle that underscores the role of habits in shaping our lives and determining our level of personal achievement. It recognizes that our habits, both conscious and unconscious, exert a powerful influence on our thoughts, actions, and outcomes.

At its core, the Law of Cosmic Habitforce suggests that our habits are not merely random behaviors but rather deeply ingrained patterns of thought and action that govern our daily lives. These habits are formed through repeated actions and reinforced by the feedback loops of our experiences.

By understanding and harnessing the Law of Cosmic Habitforce, we can deliberately cultivate habits that support our goals and aspirations, leading to greater success and fulfillment. This involves identifying the habits that are serving us well and consciously reinforcing them, while also identifying habits that are holding us back and taking steps to break free from them.

The Law of Cosmic Habitforce emphasizes the importance of consistency and discipline in habit formation. It recognizes that small, incremental changes, practiced consistently over time, can lead to significant improvements in our lives. By committing to positive habits and routines, we can create a momentum that propels us towards our goals with ever-increasing speed and efficiency.

Additionally, the Law of Cosmic Habit Force highlights the interconnectedness of our habits with the broader forces of the universe. It suggests that our habits are not isolated phenomena but rather part of a larger cosmic order that governs the workings of the universe. By aligning our habits with the natural rhythms and laws of the cosmos, we can tap into a source of energy and inspiration that transcends our individual efforts.

In essence, the Law of Cosmic Habit Force is the science of personal achievement—a systematic approach to understanding and harnessing the power of habits to create the life we desire. By mastering our habits and aligning them with our goals, we can unlock our full potential and achieve extraordinary levels of success and fulfillment in all areas of our lives

The Law of Cosmic Habitforce is a powerful principle that governs the patterns of behavior and thought that shape our lives. It is based on the idea that our habits, whether positive or negative, have a profound impact on our success and personal fulfillment.

According to this law, our habits are not merely random behaviors; they are deeply ingrained patterns that govern our thoughts, feelings, and actions. These habits are formed through repetition and reinforcement, often without conscious awareness. Over time, they become deeply embedded in our subconscious mind, influencing our behavior on a subconscious level.

The Law of Cosmic Habitforce states that by consciously cultivating positive habits and eliminating negative ones, we can harness the power of habit to achieve our goals and create the life we desire. This requires self-discipline, consistency, and a willingness to challenge old patterns of thinking and behavior.

To leverage the Law of Cosmic Habitforce in our favor, we must first identify the habits that are holding us back from achieving our full potential. This may involve self-reflection, introspection, and honest evaluation of our strengths and weaknesses. Once we have identified these negative habits, we can begin the process of replacing them with positive ones.

Positive habits are the building blocks of personal achievement. They empower us to take consistent action towards our goals, overcome obstacles, and stay focused on our priorities. Whether it's establishing a daily exercise routine, practicing gratitude, or cultivating a growth mindset, positive habits create the foundation for success in all areas of life.

The key to harnessing the power of the Law of Cosmic Habitforce lies in repetition and consistency. By consistently practicing positive habits, we reinforce neural pathways in our brain and strengthen the connections associated with those behaviors. Over time, these habits become automatic and effortless, making personal achievement and success a natural outcome.

In the words of Napoleon Hill, "Cherish your visions and your dreams as they are the children of your soul, the blueprints of your ultimate achievements."

48

48

How to Develop the "X-Factor": Personal Magnetism

The "X-Factor," often referred to as personal magnetism, is that intangible quality that makes certain individuals stand out and attract others to them effortlessly. It is a combination of charisma, confidence, and authenticity that exudes from within and captivates those around them. Developing the "X-Factor" can enhance your presence, influence, and impact in both personal and professional settings. Here are some strategies to cultivate personal magnetism:

1. Self-Confidence: Confidence is the foundation of personal magnetism. Believe in yourself and your abilities, and project that confidence outwardly through your body language, tone of voice, and demeanor. Stand tall, make eye contact, and speak with conviction. Confidence is contagious and will naturally draw others to you.
2. Authenticity: Authenticity is key to developing personal magnetism. Be genuine and true to yourself, rather than trying to emulate someone else. Embrace your unique qualities, quirks, and imperfections, and let your true personality shine through. Authenticity creates a genuine connection with others and fosters trust and rapport.
3. Positive Attitude: Cultivate a positive attitude and outlook on life. Focus

on the good in yourself and others, and approach every situation with optimism and enthusiasm. Smile often, laugh freely, and radiate positive energy. A positive attitude is infectious and will attract like-minded individuals to you.

4. Charisma: Charisma is the ability to charm and inspire others with your presence and personality. Develop your charisma by honing your communication skills, listening attentively, and showing genuine interest in others. Use humor, storytelling, and emotional intelligence to engage and captivate your audience. Charisma is a magnetic quality that draws people to you and leaves a lasting impression.
5. Self-Awareness: Self-awareness is essential for cultivating personal magnetism. Know your strengths, weaknesses, and areas for growth, and strive to continually improve and evolve. Be mindful of your thoughts, emotions, and behaviors, and how they impact those around you. Self-awareness allows you to project authenticity and confidence, which are attractive qualities in any individual.
6. Empathy and Empathy: Show empathy and compassion towards others, and strive to understand their perspectives, feelings, and needs. Empathy creates a deep emotional connection and fosters trust and rapport. Practice active listening, validate others' experiences, and offer support and encouragement when needed. Empathy is a powerful force that strengthens relationships and enhances personal magnetism.

By incorporating these strategies into your daily life, you can cultivate the "X-Factor" and develop personal magnetism that draws others to you effortlessly. Remember to be confident, authentic, positive, charismatic, self-aware, and empathetic in your interactions with others. With practice and intention, you can enhance your presence, influence, and impact and become a magnetic force in any situation.

Personal magnetism, often referred to as the "X-Factor," is a quality that sets certain individuals apart and draws others to them like a magnet. It's a combination of charisma, confidence, and authenticity that makes people stand out in a crowd and leaves a lasting impression on those they encounter.

HOW TO DEVELOP THE "X-FACTOR": PERSONAL MAGNETISM

While some may seem to possess this quality naturally, personal magnetism is something that can be developed and cultivated over time. Here's how:

1. Confidence: Confidence is at the core of personal magnetism. Believe in yourself and your abilities, and others will be drawn to your self-assurance. Practice positive self-talk, set and achieve goals, and step out of your comfort zone regularly to build your confidence muscle.
2. Authenticity: Authenticity is essential for cultivating personal magnetism. Be genuine, sincere, and true to yourself in all your interactions. People are naturally drawn to those who are authentic and transparent, so don't be afraid to let your true self shine through.
3. Charisma: Charisma is a combination of charm, charisma, and presence that captivates others. Cultivate your charisma by practicing active listening, maintaining eye contact, and being genuinely interested in others. Use humor, storytelling, and body language to engage and captivate your audience.
4. Positive energy: Positive energy is infectious and can instantly attract others to you. Cultivate a positive mindset, radiate enthusiasm, and focus on the good in every situation. Smile often, express gratitude, and be generous with your compliments and encouragement.
5. Emotional intelligence: Emotional intelligence is the ability to understand and manage your emotions and the emotions of others. Develop your emotional intelligence by practicing empathy, active listening, and effective communication skills. Be attuned to the needs and feelings of others, and respond with kindness and compassion.
6. Charismatic body language: Body language plays a significant role in personal magnetism. Stand tall, make eye contact, and use confident, open gestures to convey your message. Pay attention to your posture, facial expressions, and tone of voice to ensure they are aligned with your message and intentions.
7. Continuous self-improvement: Personal magnetism is not a static quality; it requires continuous self-improvement and growth. Invest in your personal and professional development, seek feedback from others,

THE POWER

and strive to become the best version of yourself. Embrace challenges as opportunities for growth and learning, and never stop evolving and improving.

By developing these qualities and practices, you can cultivate personal magnetism and unleash your "X-Factor" to attract and inspire others. Remember that personal magnetism is not about being perfect; it's about being authentic, confident, and genuinely interested in others. With practice and persistence, you can develop the charisma and presence that will set you apart and leave a lasting impression wherever you go.

49

49

the "Miracle" of Your Mind: Unlocking Infinite Potential

The human mind is a remarkable and mysterious instrument capable of incredible feats. Often referred to as the "miracle" of the mind, its potential is virtually limitless, waiting to be unlocked and harnessed for personal growth and achievement.

At its core, the "miracle" of the mind lies in its capacity for imagination, creativity, and innovation. It is the source of our thoughts, beliefs, and emotions, shaping our perceptions of the world and influencing our actions and behaviors. By understanding and tapping into the power of our minds, we can unlock infinite possibilities and transform our lives in profound ways.

One of the key aspects of unlocking the "miracle" of the mind is harnessing the power of visualization. Visualization is the process of mentally picturing our goals and desires as if they have already been achieved. By vividly imagining our desired outcomes, we activate the creative forces of the mind and align ourselves with the energy of manifestation. Through regular practice of visualization, we can program our subconscious mind to attract and create the circumstances necessary for our success.

Another essential aspect of unlocking the "miracle" of the mind is cultivating a positive mindset and belief system. Our thoughts and beliefs have a profound impact on our reality, shaping our experiences and influencing our outcomes. By cultivating a mindset of positivity, optimism, and abundance, we can reprogram our subconscious mind to support our goals and aspirations. Through affirmations, positive self-talk, and gratitude practices, we can shift our focus from limitations to possibilities and open ourselves up to a world of infinite potential.

Additionally, mindfulness and meditation are powerful tools for unlocking the "miracle" of the mind. By quieting the chatter of the conscious mind and tuning into the present moment, we can tap into the deeper wisdom and intuition of our subconscious mind. Through regular practice of mindfulness and meditation, we can cultivate a deeper connection with ourselves and gain insight into our true desires and purpose in life.

In the words of Napoleon Hill, "What the mind can conceive and believe, it can achieve." The "miracle" of the mind lies in its ability to conceive of infinite possibilities and bring them into reality through focused intention and belief. By unlocking the potential of our minds and harnessing the creative forces within us, we can achieve anything we set our minds to and create the life of our dreams.

The human mind is a miraculous instrument capable of incredible feats of creativity, innovation, and discovery. It is the seat of consciousness, the source of our thoughts, beliefs, and perceptions, and the gateway to infinite possibilities. When we tap into the power of our minds and unlock their full potential, we can achieve extraordinary things and create the life we desire.

The "miracle" of your mind lies in its inherent capacity for growth, adaptation, and transformation. Unlike any other known phenomenon in the universe, the human mind has the ability to learn, evolve, and expand its horizons indefinitely. It is not bound by the constraints of time, space, or circumstance but is limited only by the boundaries of our imagination and belief.

To unlock the infinite potential of your mind, it's essential to cultivate a mindset of curiosity, openness, and possibility. Approach life with a sense of wonder and awe, embracing new experiences and challenges as opportunities for growth and discovery. Be willing to explore new ideas, perspectives, and ways of thinking, and allow yourself to be inspired by the world around you.

Belief is a powerful catalyst for unlocking the potential of your mind. Believe in your ability to learn, grow, and overcome obstacles. Cultivate a positive mindset, and affirm your belief in your own capabilities and potential. Replace limiting beliefs with empowering ones, and envision yourself achieving your goals and dreams with clarity and conviction.

Visualization is a potent tool for harnessing the power of your mind and manifesting your desires. Take time each day to visualize your goals and aspirations as if they have already been achieved. Engage all your senses and emotions, and immerse yourself fully in the experience of success and fulfillment. By consistently reinforcing positive mental images, you can program your subconscious mind for success and attract the resources and opportunities you need to bring your vision to life.

Self-awareness is essential for unlocking the potential of your mind. Take time to reflect on your thoughts, emotions, and behaviors, and identify any patterns or beliefs that may be holding you back. Practice mindfulness and meditation to quiet the chatter of the mind and connect with your inner wisdom and intuition. By developing a deeper understanding of yourself, you can align your thoughts and actions with your true desires and aspirations.

In the words of Napoleon Hill, "Whatever the mind can conceive and believe, it can achieve." The "miracle" of your mind lies in its boundless potential to create, innovate, and transform. By harnessing the power of your mind and unlocking its infinite potential, you can transcend limitations, overcome obstacles, and create a life of purpose, passion, and fulfillment.

THE POWER

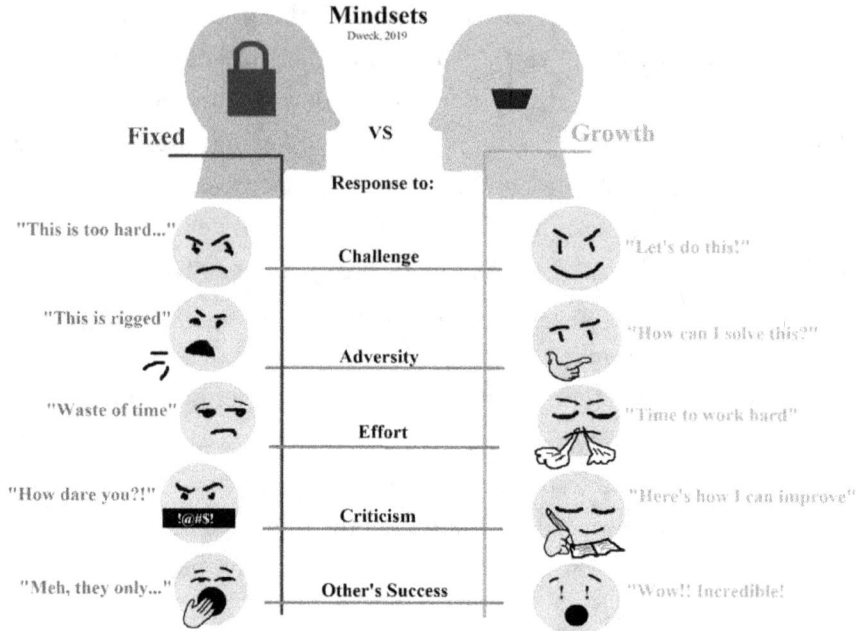

50

50

How to Transform Failures into Stepping Stones for Success

Failure is an inevitable part of life, but it does not have to define us or dictate our future. Instead of seeing failure as the end of the road, we can choose to view it as a valuable learning experience and an opportunity for growth. By transforming failures into stepping stones for success, we can turn setbacks into springboards for achieving our goals and dreams. Here's how:

1. Embrace a Growth Mindset: Adopt a growth mindset, which sees failures as opportunities for learning and growth rather than setbacks. Understand that failure is a natural part of the learning process and that each setback brings valuable lessons and insights that can help you succeed in the future.
2. Analyze the Failure: Take time to reflect on the failure and analyze what went wrong. Identify the factors that contributed to the failure, whether they were external circumstances or internal factors within your control. Be honest with yourself and take responsibility for your role in the outcome.
3. Learn from Mistakes: Use failure as an opportunity to learn from your mistakes and improve yourself. Take note of the lessons learned from the

experience and use them to make better decisions in the future. Embrace a growth mindset, which sees failures as opportunities for learning and growth rather than setbacks.
4. Stay Resilient: Develop resilience in the face of failure by bouncing back quickly and remaining determined to pursue your goals. Understand that setbacks are temporary and that success often requires perseverance and resilience. Use failure as motivation to work harder and keep moving forward.
5. Reframe Failure: Reframe failure as a necessary step on the path to success. Understand that many successful people have experienced failure on their journey and that setbacks are often a sign that you are pushing yourself outside of your comfort zone. Use failure as fuel to drive you towards greater success.
6. Focus on Solutions: Instead of dwelling on the failure, focus on finding solutions and taking proactive steps to move forward. Break down your goals into smaller, actionable steps and create a plan to overcome obstacles and achieve success. Maintain a positive attitude and believe in your ability to overcome challenges.
7. Celebrate Progress: Celebrate your progress and achievements, no matter how small. Recognize that every step forward, no matter how small, is a victory on the path to success. Use positive reinforcement to motivate yourself and build momentum towards your goals.

By transforming failures into stepping stones for success, we can turn setbacks into opportunities for growth and achievement. Embrace failure as a natural part of the learning process, learn from your mistakes, and remain resilient in the face of adversity. With determination, perseverance, and a positive mindset, you can overcome obstacles and achieve your goals, turning your dreams into reality.

Failure is an inevitable part of the journey towards success, but it is how we respond to failure that ultimately determines our trajectory. Instead of allowing failure to discourage or defeat us, we can choose to see it as an opportunity for growth, learning, and resilience. Here's how to transform

HOW TO TRANSFORM FAILURES INTO STEPPING STONES FOR SUCCESS

failures into stepping stones for success:

1. Embrace a Growth Mindset: Adopt a growth mindset, which views failure as a natural and necessary part of the learning process. Instead of seeing failure as evidence of personal inadequacy, see it as an opportunity to learn, grow, and improve. Cultivate a mindset of resilience, perseverance, and optimism that enables you to bounce back from setbacks stronger than before.
2. Reframe Failure as Feedback: Instead of viewing failure as a final outcome, see it as feedback that provides valuable insights and information. Ask yourself what you can learn from the experience and how you can use that knowledge to improve and adapt. Every failure contains seeds of wisdom and opportunity that can help you refine your approach and move closer to success.
3. Focus on Lessons Learned: Rather than dwelling on the disappointment or frustration of failure, focus on the lessons learned and the progress made. Take time to reflect on what went wrong, what could have been done differently, and what you can do better next time. Use failure as a springboard for growth and development, turning setbacks into opportunities for self-improvement and mastery.
4. Cultivate Resilience: Resilience is the ability to bounce back from adversity and overcome challenges with grace and determination. Cultivate resilience by developing coping strategies, building a strong support network, and maintaining a positive outlook in the face of setbacks. Remember that setbacks are temporary and that every failure brings you one step closer to success.
5. Set Realistic Expectations: Unrealistic expectations can set you up for failure and disappointment. Set realistic, achievable goals that stretch your abilities but are within reach with effort and perseverance. Break larger goals down into smaller, manageable steps, and celebrate each milestone along the way. By setting realistic expectations, you set yourself up for success and minimize the risk of failure.
6. Stay Persistent: Success rarely comes overnight, and setbacks are

inevitable on the path to achievement. Stay persistent and committed to your goals, even in the face of adversity. Use failure as motivation to work harder, smarter, and more strategically towards your goals. Remember that every successful person has faced setbacks and failures along the way—it's how they respond to those challenges that sets them apart.

7. Keep Moving Forward: Finally, don't let failure hold you back or derail your progress. Accept failure as a natural part of the journey and keep moving forward with determination and resilience. Use failure as fuel to propel you towards your goals, knowing that each setback brings you one step closer to success. With perseverance, resilience, and a growth mindset, you can transform failures into stepping stones for success and achieve your dreams.

HOW TO TRANSFORM FAILURES INTO STEPPING STONES FOR SUCCESS

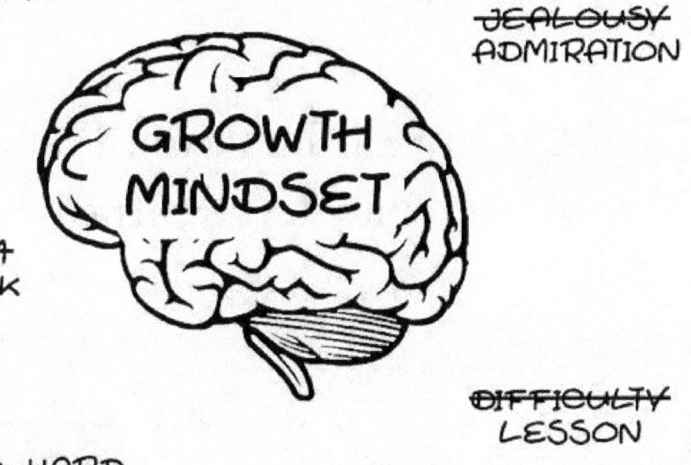

51

51

The Magic of Enthusiasm: Fueling Your Journey to Greatness

Enthusiasm is a potent force that ignites passion, energy, and excitement in everything we do. It is the spark that fuels our journey to greatness, propelling us forward with purpose and determination. When we approach life with enthusiasm, we tap into a boundless source of motivation and inspiration that empowers us to achieve our highest aspirations. Here's how to harness the magic of enthusiasm to fuel your journey to greatness:

1. Cultivate Passion: Passion is the fuel that powers enthusiasm. Discover what you love and what excites you, and pursue it with unwavering passion and dedication. Whether it's a hobby, a career, or a cause, immerse yourself fully in activities that ignite your enthusiasm and bring you joy and fulfillment.
2. Find Your Why: Connect with your purpose and values to fuel your enthusiasm. Understand why your goals and aspirations are meaningful to you and how they align with your values and vision for your life. When you have a clear sense of purpose, you'll find that enthusiasm comes naturally as you work towards your goals with passion and conviction.
3. Stay Positive: Maintain a positive outlook and focus on the possibilities

rather than the obstacles. Cultivate gratitude, optimism, and resilience in the face of challenges, and look for opportunities for growth and learning in every situation. A positive attitude not only fuels enthusiasm but also attracts positive outcomes and opportunities into your life.

4. Embrace Curiosity: Approach life with a sense of curiosity and wonder, and be open to new experiences and opportunities. Ask questions, seek knowledge, and explore new ideas and perspectives. Curiosity fuels enthusiasm by keeping your mind engaged and your spirit alive with the excitement of discovery and exploration.

5. Surround Yourself with Enthusiasm: Surround yourself with people who share your enthusiasm and passion for life. Seek out positive, energetic individuals who inspire and uplift you, and avoid negativity and pessimism. Engage in activities and environments that energize and motivate you, whether it's spending time in nature, pursuing creative endeavors, or participating in community events.

6. Take Action: Enthusiasm is not just a feeling; it's a call to action. Channel your enthusiasm into concrete steps towards your goals and aspirations. Break down your goals into manageable tasks and take consistent, focused action towards achieving them. As you make progress and see results, your enthusiasm will only continue to grow, fueling your journey to greatness.

7. Spread Joy and Inspiration: Share your enthusiasm with others and inspire them to pursue their own greatness. Be a source of positivity, encouragement, and motivation for those around you, and celebrate their successes as enthusiastically as you celebrate your own. By spreading joy and inspiration, you amplify the magic of enthusiasm and create a ripple effect of greatness in the world.

In the words of Ralph Waldo Emerson, "Nothing great was ever achieved without enthusiasm." Embrace the magic of enthusiasm, and let it fuel your journey to greatness. With passion, purpose, and positivity as your guiding lights, there's no limit to what you can achieve and no obstacle you can't overcome.

Enthusiasm is a powerful force that propels us towards our goals, infusing our actions with passion, energy, and excitement. It is the spark that ignites our ambitions, the fuel that sustains us through challenges, and the magnet that attracts success and opportunities into our lives. When we approach life with enthusiasm, we unleash our full potential and embark on a journey towards greatness.

Enthusiasm is contagious—it inspires others, motivates them to action, and creates a ripple effect of positivity and momentum. When we are enthusiastic about our goals and aspirations, we inspire those around us to believe in themselves and their own potential. Our enthusiasm becomes a beacon of hope and possibility, lighting the way for others to follow.

But enthusiasm is more than just a fleeting emotion—it is a mindset, a way of approaching life with passion, purpose, and determination. It is a conscious choice to embrace life with open arms, to pursue our dreams with unwavering commitment, and to greet each day with optimism and enthusiasm.

To harness the magic of enthusiasm, it's essential to align our goals and actions with our passions and values. When we pursue goals that are meaningful and inspiring to us, enthusiasm comes naturally, fueling our journey with purpose and excitement. Take time to reflect on what truly excites and energizes you, and channel that enthusiasm into your pursuits.

Cultivate gratitude for the opportunities and blessings in your life, and approach each day with a sense of wonder and appreciation. Even in the face of challenges and setbacks, maintain a positive outlook and focus on the potential for growth and learning. By embracing a mindset of gratitude and positivity, you can cultivate enthusiasm as a way of life.

Surround yourself with positive influences and like-minded individuals who share your passion and enthusiasm for life. Seek out mentors, role models, and supportive communities that inspire and encourage you to pursue your dreams with zeal and determination. Collaboration and camaraderie can amplify the magic of enthusiasm, creating a supportive network of allies and cheerleaders to fuel your journey to greatness.

Finally, take inspired action towards your goals, fueled by the fire of enthusiasm burning within you. Break down your goals into manageable steps, and approach each task with enthusiasm and energy. Celebrate your progress and achievements along the way, and use setbacks as opportunities to rekindle your enthusiasm and refocus your efforts.

52

52

The Golden Rule: The Principle of Mutual Benefit

The Golden Rule, often expressed as "treat others as you would like to be treated," is a timeless principle that transcends cultures, religions, and philosophies. At its core, the Golden Rule embodies the principle of mutual benefit—the idea that our actions towards others should be guided by empathy, kindness, and respect, with the understanding that what we give out into the world will ultimately come back to us.

When we practice the Golden Rule, we create a ripple effect of positivity and goodwill that enriches not only our own lives but also the lives of those around us. By treating others with compassion, fairness, and understanding, we foster harmonious relationships, build trust and mutual respect, and contribute to a more compassionate and caring world.

The Golden Rule invites us to put ourselves in the shoes of others and consider how our actions and words impact their lives. It encourages us to act with integrity, honesty, and sincerity, knowing that our behavior towards others reflects our own values and character. Whether in our personal relationships, our professional interactions, or our interactions with strangers, the Golden Rule serves as a guiding principle for ethical and moral conduct.

Practicing the Golden Rule requires empathy—the ability to understand

and share the feelings of others. By empathizing with others' perspectives, experiences, and emotions, we can respond with compassion and sensitivity, fostering deeper connections and fostering a sense of belonging and acceptance.

The Golden Rule also emphasizes the importance of reciprocity—the idea that the kindness and generosity we extend to others will be returned to us in some form. When we act with generosity, compassion, and goodwill, we create a positive energy that attracts similar blessings and opportunities into our own lives. Conversely, when we act with cruelty, selfishness, or indifference, we sow seeds of discord and negativity that can come back to haunt us.

In a world often characterized by division, conflict, and discord, the Golden Rule serves as a beacon of hope and unity—a reminder of our shared humanity and interconnectedness. By embodying the principle of mutual benefit and treating others with kindness, respect, and compassion, we can create a more harmonious and inclusive world where everyone has the opportunity to thrive and flourish.

In the words of Mahatma Gandhi, "The best way to find yourself is to lose yourself in the service of others." By living by the Golden Rule and seeking to benefit others, we not only enrich the lives of those around us but also discover our own true purpose and fulfillment. Let us strive to make the Golden Rule the guiding principle of our lives, and watch as it transforms our world for the better.

The Golden Rule is a timeless principle that transcends cultures, religions, and generations. It is a simple yet profound concept that encourages us to treat others as we would like to be treated ourselves. At its core, the Golden Rule embodies the principle of mutual benefit—the idea that by treating others with kindness, respect, and empathy, we create a ripple effect of goodwill and harmony that benefits everyone involved.

The Golden Rule encourages us to cultivate compassion and empathy for others, recognizing their inherent worth and dignity as fellow human beings. It reminds us to consider the impact of our words and actions on others and to strive to make choices that uplift and empower those around us. By embodying the Golden Rule in our interactions with others, we create a positive and supportive environment where everyone can thrive.

At its heart, the Golden Rule is about reciprocity and mutual benefit. When we treat others with kindness, understanding, and generosity, we not only improve their lives but also enhance our own. By fostering positive relationships and building trust and goodwill with others, we create a network of support and collaboration that enriches our lives and opens doors of opportunity.

The Golden Rule also extends beyond individual interactions to encompass broader social and ethical considerations. It calls on us to strive for fairness, justice, and equality in our communities and institutions, recognizing that we are all interconnected and interdependent. By upholding the principles of fairness and equity, we create a more just and compassionate society where everyone has the opportunity to thrive.

Practicing the Golden Rule requires mindfulness, empathy, and a willingness to see the world from others' perspectives. It involves actively listening to others, seeking to understand their needs and concerns, and responding with compassion and kindness. By cultivating these qualities, we can create meaningful connections and build bridges of understanding that transcend differences and unite us in our common humanity.

In a world often characterized by division, conflict, and mistrust, the Golden Rule offers a beacon of hope and guidance. It reminds us that we are all part of a larger human family, bound together by our shared humanity and our common aspirations for a better world. By embracing the principle of mutual benefit and embodying the Golden Rule in our daily lives, we can create a more compassionate, inclusive, and harmonious world for ourselves and future generations.

THE GOLDEN RULE: THE PRINCIPLE OF MUTUAL BENEFIT

53

53

The Four Pillars of Leadership: Defining Your Path to Influence

Leadership is a multifaceted concept that encompasses a wide range of qualities and skills. At its core, effective leadership is built upon four foundational pillars that define the path to influence and impact. These pillars serve as guiding principles for aspiring leaders, providing a framework for personal and professional growth. Let's explore each of the four pillars in detail:

1. Vision: Vision is the cornerstone of effective leadership. It involves having a clear sense of purpose and direction, and the ability to articulate a compelling vision of the future. A strong vision inspires and motivates others, rallying them around a common goal and guiding their actions towards its realization. As a leader, it's essential to communicate your vision with clarity and passion, and to engage others in its pursuit.
2. Integrity: Integrity is the foundation of trust and credibility in leadership. It involves acting with honesty, fairness, and transparency, and adhering to a set of ethical principles and values. Leaders who demonstrate integrity earn the trust and respect of those they lead, fostering a culture of trust and accountability within their organizations. Integrity requires consistency between words and actions, and a commitment to doing

what is right, even when it is difficult or unpopular.
3. Influence: Influence is the ability to inspire and empower others to take action and achieve common goals. It involves building strong relationships, communicating effectively, and leading by example. Leaders who wield influence are able to motivate and persuade others, even in the absence of formal authority. They are adept at building consensus, resolving conflicts, and driving positive change within their organizations and communities.
4. Resilience: Resilience is the capacity to bounce back from setbacks, adapt to change, and persevere in the face of adversity. It involves maintaining a positive attitude, staying focused on goals, and learning from failures and setbacks. Resilient leaders are able to navigate challenges with grace and composure, inspiring confidence and stability in those they lead. They view obstacles as opportunities for growth and innovation, and remain steadfast in their commitment to achieving their vision.

By cultivating these four pillars of leadership—vision, integrity, influence, and resilience—individuals can define their path to influence and impact. Whether leading teams, organizations, or communities, effective leaders embody these principles in their words and actions, inspiring others to reach their full potential and achieve collective success.

Leadership is not just about holding a title or position of authority; it's about inspiring and empowering others to achieve their full potential and work towards a common goal. The Four Pillars of Leadership represent the essential qualities and attributes that define effective leadership and guide individuals on their path to influence. These pillars serve as the foundation upon which successful leaders build their vision, inspire others, and drive positive change.

1. Vision: Vision is the cornerstone of effective leadership. It involves having a clear sense of purpose and direction, and the ability to articulate a compelling vision for the future. A strong vision inspires and motivates others, providing a sense of purpose and direction that guides their

actions and decisions. Effective leaders communicate their vision with passion and conviction, rallying others around a shared goal and inspiring them to work towards its realization.

2. Integrity: Integrity is the bedrock of trust and credibility in leadership. It involves honesty, transparency, and a commitment to ethical behavior in all aspects of leadership. Leaders with integrity demonstrate consistency between their words and actions, earning the trust and respect of those they lead. They lead by example, upholding high ethical standards and treating others with fairness, respect, and dignity.

3. Empowerment: Empowerment is about enabling others to unleash their full potential and contribute their unique talents and perspectives to the team. Effective leaders empower their team members by providing support, encouragement, and opportunities for growth and development. They foster a culture of trust, collaboration, and innovation, where individuals feel valued, empowered, and motivated to take ownership of their work and contribute to the collective success.

4. Resilience: Resilience is the ability to adapt, persevere, and thrive in the face of challenges and setbacks. Effective leaders demonstrate resilience by maintaining a positive outlook, staying focused on their goals, and bouncing back from adversity with strength and determination. They lead by example, showing resilience in the face of adversity and inspiring others to do the same. They remain calm and composed under pressure, and they use setbacks as opportunities for growth and learning.

By embracing the Four Pillars of Leadership—vision, integrity, empowerment, and resilience—individuals can define their path to influence and make a positive impact in their organizations, communities, and beyond. These pillars serve as guiding principles for effective leadership, providing a roadmap for inspiring others, driving change, and achieving shared goals. As leaders cultivate these qualities and attributes, they can create a culture of excellence, innovation, and collaboration that empowers individuals and teams to achieve their full potential and create a brighter future for all.

Human Survival Mindset

54

How to Build Self-Confidence and Overcome Self-Consciousness

Self-confidence is essential for success and fulfillment in all areas of life, yet many people struggle with feelings of self-consciousness and inadequacy. Building self-confidence involves cultivating a positive self-image, embracing your strengths, and learning to silence your inner critic. Here are some strategies to help you build self-confidence and overcome self-consciousness:

1. Identify Your Strengths: Take stock of your unique talents, skills, and accomplishments. Make a list of your strengths and achievements, and remind yourself of them regularly. Focus on what you do well and what sets you apart from others. Celebrate your successes and use them as evidence of your capabilities and potential.
2. Set Realistic Goals: Set achievable goals that stretch your abilities but are within reach with effort and perseverance. Break larger goals down into smaller, manageable steps, and celebrate each milestone along the way. By setting and achieving goals, you build confidence in your ability to succeed and overcome challenges.
3. Practice Self-Compassion: Be kind to yourself and treat yourself with the same compassion and understanding that you would extend to a friend.

Accept that nobody is perfect, and it's okay to make mistakes or fall short sometimes. Instead of dwelling on your perceived flaws or shortcomings, focus on your progress and efforts towards self-improvement.

4. Challenge Negative Self-Talk: Pay attention to your internal dialogue and challenge negative thoughts and beliefs about yourself. Replace self-critical thoughts with more balanced and realistic ones. Instead of saying, "I can't do this," say, "I'm capable of figuring this out." By changing your self-talk, you can rewire your brain to be more positive and supportive.
5. Step Out of Your Comfort Zone: Growth and self-confidence come from pushing past your comfort zone and trying new things. Take on challenges that scare you or make you feel uncomfortable, and embrace the opportunity to learn and grow. Each time you step outside your comfort zone and succeed, your confidence grows stronger.
6. Practice Assertiveness: Assertiveness is the ability to express your thoughts, feelings, and needs in a clear and respectful manner. Practice asserting yourself in situations where you feel self-conscious or uncertain. Start with small, low-stakes interactions, and gradually work your way up to more challenging situations. By advocating for yourself and standing up for your rights, you build confidence in your ability to assert yourself in any situation.
7. Surround Yourself with Supportive People: Surround yourself with positive, supportive people who believe in you and encourage you to be your best self. Seek out mentors, friends, and family members who uplift and inspire you, and minimize time spent with people who bring you down or undermine your confidence.

Building self-confidence is a journey that takes time, patience, and practice. By implementing these strategies and committing to your personal growth, you can overcome self-consciousness and develop the self-confidence you need to thrive in all areas of your life. Remember that you are capable, deserving, and worthy of success and happiness, and embrace the journey towards becoming your most confident self.\

Self-confidence is a key ingredient for success and fulfillment in life, yet many people struggle with feelings of self-doubt and self-consciousness. Fortunately, self-confidence is a skill that can be cultivated and strengthened over time. Here are some strategies to help you build self-confidence and overcome self-consciousness:

1. Practice self-compassion: Treat yourself with kindness and compassion, especially when facing challenges or setbacks. Acknowledge your strengths and accomplishments, and be gentle with yourself when things don't go as planned. Practice positive self-talk and challenge negative thoughts and beliefs that undermine your confidence.
2. Set realistic goals: Set achievable goals that stretch your abilities but are within reach with effort and perseverance. Break larger goals down into smaller, manageable steps, and celebrate each milestone along the way. By setting and achieving goals, you build confidence in your ability to succeed.
3. Focus on your strengths: Identify your strengths, talents, and areas of expertise, and focus on developing and leveraging them to your advantage. Recognize the value you bring to the table and embrace your unique qualities and abilities. By focusing on your strengths, you build confidence in your abilities and contributions.
4. Step out of your comfort zone: Challenge yourself to step out of your comfort zone and try new things, even if they feel intimidating or uncomfortable at first. Embrace opportunities for growth and learning, and be willing to take risks and make mistakes along the way. Each time you push past your comfort zone, you build confidence in your ability to handle challenges and adapt to new situations.
5. Practice assertiveness: Assertiveness involves expressing your thoughts, feelings, and needs in a clear and respectful manner, without being passive or aggressive. Practice assertive communication skills, such as speaking up for yourself, setting boundaries, and advocating for your interests. By asserting yourself in a positive and confident manner, you build self-confidence and assertiveness.

6. Cultivate a positive mindset: Cultivate a positive mindset by focusing on the present moment and practicing gratitude for the blessings in your life. Surround yourself with positive influences and supportive relationships that uplift and encourage you. Challenge negative self-talk and replace it with affirmations and positive affirmations that bolster your confidence and self-esteem.
7. Seek support: Don't be afraid to seek support from friends, family, or a trusted mentor or coach when you're struggling with self-confidence. Surround yourself with people who believe in you and encourage you to reach your full potential. By building a support network of positive influences, you can overcome self-consciousness and build self-confidence.

Building self-confidence takes time, effort, and practice, but the rewards are well worth it. By adopting these strategies and committing to your personal growth and development, you can overcome self-consciousness and build the self-confidence you need to thrive in all areas of your life. Believe in yourself and your abilities, and remember that you are capable of achieving great things.

55

55

The Power of Imagination: Creating Your Reality

Imagination is a remarkable gift that allows us to transcend the limits of our physical reality and explore the boundless realms of possibility. It is the creative force that fuels innovation, inspires invention, and drives progress in every aspect of human endeavor. Imagination has the power to shape our perceptions, influence our beliefs, and ultimately create our reality.

At its core, imagination is the ability to conceive of things that do not yet exist—to envision new worlds, new ideas, and new possibilities. It is the spark of creativity that ignites our passions, drives our curiosity, and fuels our dreams. Imagination empowers us to break free from the constraints of the present moment and envision a future that is limited only by the boundaries of our imagination.

The power of imagination lies in its ability to transform our thoughts into reality. When we imagine something vividly and with conviction, we activate the creative forces of the mind and set in motion a series of events that can lead to its manifestation. Imagination allows us to visualize our goals, dreams, and aspirations as if they have already been achieved, thereby aligning our thoughts and actions with our desired outcomes.

Imagination is also a potent tool for problem-solving and innovation. By envisioning new possibilities and exploring alternative perspectives, we can overcome obstacles, navigate challenges, and discover innovative solutions to complex problems. Imagination encourages us to think outside the box, challenge conventional wisdom, and push the boundaries of what is possible.

But perhaps the most profound power of imagination lies in its ability to shape our beliefs and perceptions of reality. The stories we tell ourselves, the images we hold in our minds, and the beliefs we internalize all influence the reality we experience. By harnessing the power of imagination, we can rewrite the script of our lives, reframe our experiences, and create a reality that aligns with our deepest desires and aspirations.

In the words of Albert Einstein, "Imagination is more important than knowledge. For knowledge is limited, whereas imagination embraces the entire world, stimulating progress, giving birth to evolution." By embracing the power of imagination and nurturing our creative spirit, we can unlock new possibilities, unleash our full potential, and create a reality that is limited only by the boundaries of our imagination.

Imagination is a remarkable faculty of the human mind that allows us to envision possibilities, explore creativity, and shape our reality. It is the spark that ignites innovation, fuels inspiration, and unlocks the door to endless possibilities. By harnessing the power of imagination, we can transform our dreams into reality and create the life we desire.

Imagination is more than just daydreaming or fantasizing—it is a powerful tool for visualization and manifestation. When we imagine a desired outcome or goal with clarity and intention, we activate the creative forces of the mind and set in motion a series of events that align with our vision. Imagination allows us to see beyond the limitations of the present moment and envision a future that is filled with possibility and potential.

The power of imagination lies in its ability to transcend the constraints of reality and tap into the boundless realm of the mind. It allows us to explore new ideas, solve problems, and envision alternative realities that inspire and motivate us to take action. Imagination is the driving force behind innovation and progress, fueling scientific discoveries, artistic creations, and technological advancements.

To harness the power of imagination, it's essential to cultivate a sense of curiosity, wonder, and openness to new possibilities. Give yourself permission to dream big and explore the vast landscape of your imagination without limitations or constraints. Allow yourself to visualize your goals and aspirations with clarity and detail, using all of your senses to bring your vision to life.

Practice creative visualization techniques to harness the power of your imagination and manifest your desires. Close your eyes and imagine yourself achieving your goals with vivid detail, engaging all of your senses to create a rich and immersive experience. Use affirmations and positive self-talk to reinforce your vision and cultivate belief in your ability to achieve your dreams.

Imagination is a potent force for transformation and growth, but it requires nurturing and practice to fully harness its power. Set aside time each day to engage in creative activities that stimulate your imagination, such as writing, drawing, or daydreaming. Surround yourself with sources of inspiration and immerse yourself in environments that fuel your creativity and imagination.

By embracing the power of imagination, you can unlock your full potential and create a reality that is aligned with your deepest desires and aspirations. Trust in the creative forces of your mind and believe in the infinite possibilities that lie within your imagination. With imagination as your guide, you can embark on a journey of self-discovery, innovation, and transformation that leads to a life of fulfillment, joy, and abundance.

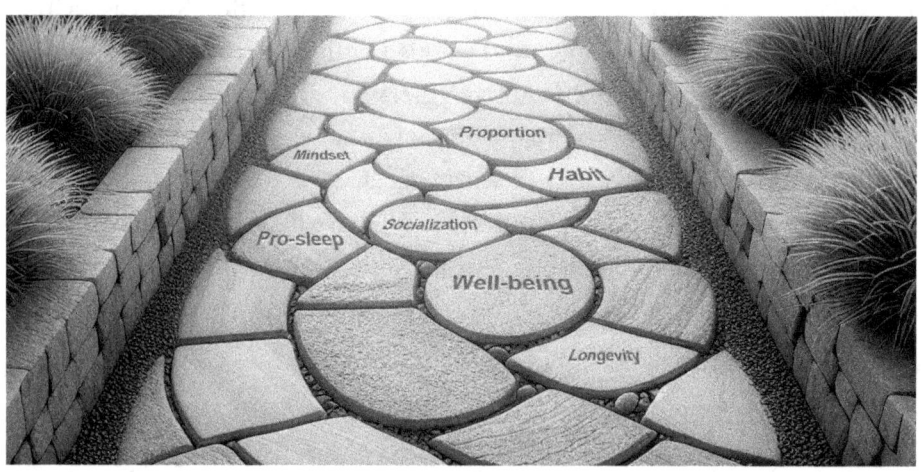

THE POWER OF IMAGINATION: CREATING YOUR REALITY

www.ingramcontent.com/pod-product-compliance
Lightning Source LLC
Chambersburg PA
CBHW052313220526
45472CB00001B/100